Our
Countryside

Editor: Barney White-Spunner
Photographer: Simon Everett

Simon Everett started supplying photos on the theme of travel to a friend's picture library whilst
serving as an Officer in the Merchant Navy. He now runs his own library and his pictures are used
widely in publications of all sorts. Passionate about the countryside and country pursuits, Simon
derives particular pleasure from this side of his work. He was born and raised in Plymouth and now
lives in Staffordshire with his wife Anna and two children.

Baily's
Chesterton Mill
French's Road
Cambridge
CB4 3NP
England
Tel 01223 350555
Fax 01223 356484

ISBN 0 9523628 4 8

Published by Baily's 1996
© Pearson Publishing Limited 1996

Reproduction by Goodfellow & Egan, Cambridge

Printed and bound by BPC Wheatons Ltd, Exeter

Contents

Preface

Our countryside is a topical subject. Many column inches and political hours have been devoted to debating it and, in the autumn of 1995, it even merited a Parliamentary White Paper in its own right. Speaking in the ensuing debate, the then Environment Secretary John Gummer said that the document showed "our determination not to allow the countryside to be turned into a museum" and how it could remain a "living, working place" without harming the environment. But what did he really mean? How many people, especially politicians, really understand what is involved in living and working in the British countryside and exactly how its 'environment' has developed?

Not many, we reckoned, and so we decided to ask people who really do understand rural issues to contribute to this book. Each contribution to *Our Countryside* represents the author's personal view. Just because someone has written one chapter it does not necessarily mean that they subscribe to the opinions expressed in other chapters. There was no editorial direction offered and, even if it had been, it would probably have been refused!

We have grouped the chapters together by content but the book does not need to be read in any particular order; it is designed to be dipped into. You will notice, however, that the same points recur. You will identify common themes: the same anxieties affect the farmer as they do the teacher; the local businessman as they do the sportsman. We hope that one of the strengths of this book is that it emphasises the commonality of the problems that our countryside faces across all spectrums of rural life.

We are not trying to make a political point as such, although individual authors understandably do so. Rather we hope that what we have done is to raise the concerns over our countryside of which we should all be aware – and about which, if we care, we will want to do something.

An idyllic view of the British countryside… but it is under severe threat

Introduction
Sir David Steel

What could be nicer than living in the British countryside? We are privileged to inhabit these varied islands where we enjoy some of the most beautiful landscapes on God's earth, rich with diverse and generally benign wildlife, and with a climate that is both comfortable to live in and conducive to agriculture. Over the centuries we have appreciated this natural gift and amplified it, developing within it our own man-made framework of woods, hedges and meadows, building attractive villages and market towns, and constructing a tolerant and happy rural society. Many people still aspire to live in the British countryside, or to retire there, confident that they will enjoy these enduring qualities of natural beauty and social comfort.

So why all the fuss? Why do we need a Countryside Movement and why am I writing the introduction to this book? Today the British countryside and its enviable way of life are under threat. It has faced severe dangers in the past – enclosures, depopulation, disease – but never before has it been confronted with such a range and concentration of threats as it is today. The major problem, and the most insidious, is us – twentieth-century British man and woman – and we are the most dangerous because we do not realise that we are a threat. Unwittingly, we are slowly unpicking the fabric that has kept our countryside special for centuries. It is ironic that in a society which prides itself on its environmental consciousness, we are unable to see the damage we are doing.

But because it is us who constitute such a threat, it is within our power to do something about it. This book seeks both to celebrate the beauty and pleasure of our countryside and to make us aware of the different ways in which we are harming it. It is not an action plan for the countryside as such but, by presenting a synthesis of views from writers with differing perspectives, it does identify common trends and problems.

Field sports have long been an emotive issue in Britain – hunting in particular – and the debate over the morality of their practice tends to obscure debate over other key matters that affect the countryside. The position of the Countryside Movement, and the editorial position of this book, is that field sports are a fundamental part of rural life and, although it is understood that many people are morally opposed to them, in a free society such as ours participation should be left to the individual conscience. I am a keen fisherman. I do not like hunting myself, but I would be uncomfortable if a society that produced men such as John Stuart Mill chose to legislate against the minority who do just because the majority now find the sport disagreeable. Some articles in this book support field sports, some do not, but none of our authors questions the individual's right to pursue them if they so choose.

I hope that once you have read this book you will be even more aware what a priceless resource our countryside and its way of life is, and that, whether you live in a high-rise block in the inner city or a croft in the Western Isles, you will be inspired to do all you can to preserve that resource – not as some rural museum but as a living, working environment of which it is a pleasure to be a part.

Happy is He Who Knows the Country Gods

Barney White-Spunner

It is not politically correct to be proud of much that is British these days, but our countryside is an exception. We are all, or very nearly all, both proud and fond of the British countryside and believe that it is the nicest in the world. Complacent? Yes, and there are many aspects of the countryside which we must certainly not be complacent about − but we are justified in indulging in a little self-satisfaction in that we were born in the British Isles, even if we have gone off British society.

God gave us the raw materials and we, as a group of peoples, have appreciated what He bestowed upon us. For a start, He saw that it was good to position our islands off the European mainland, close to the Gulf Stream, far enough north to be cool and fertile yet sufficiently far south to enjoy warm summers to ripen our crops. Consequently, He gave us a very varied climate. The old joke that the British are always talking about the weather originated precisely because our weather is so varied and that variation dictates so much of what we do. It would be unremarkable to note that it was, for example, hot in Bombay on a July morning, or that it was cold of a February evening in Murmansk, for life in those cities is structured around such certainties. Yet a warm British June is remarkable for it could mean anything from a good harvest and a thriving tourist industry, to holding the village fête or a successful wedding. Imagine the boredom of living in a country where you knew exactly what the weather was going to be like!

It is this geographical position and our varied weather that give us so much of our natural beauty and that allow us the delight of the slowly

Man and nature in perfect harmony but such views could become a thing of the past

changing seasons, the contrast in our skies or the dramatic sunsets over the western seas that we have come to love.

Nature has also blessed us with an even more varied landscape, from mountain ranges in Scotland, to the broad downland of southern England, the fens of eastern England, the valleys of Wales, the rolling grasslands of the Midlands and the moorland of the West Country, all surrounded with a wonderfully dramatic coastline, punctuated with natural harbours. We have an abundance of rivers to give us all the fresh water we could possibly need (or so it seemed until very recently), and soil in which crops grow easily.

Lastly, we share our islands with species of wildlife that have been generally helpful to us and, save the odd wolf or adder, ones which we do not have to fear, and trees and plants that are beautiful as well as being useful and edible. In short, the British Isles evolved to be as perfect a habitat for man as anywhere in the world, and consequently man migrated from his birth place in the Middle East or from the plains of Eastern Africa to find this paradise that provided such a comfortable existence. Once we arrived, we did not leave – not until our level of sophistication was so developed that affairs of the mind had become of equal importance to those of the body. Even then, when some of our ancestors sailed off to find places where they could practise their own religions or creeds, they looked for places as similar to Britain as possible.

Over the centuries we have worked our own tapestry of civilisation into this natural fabric. We have cut down and replanted the woods, grown

Man migrated from his birth place… to find this paradise that provided such a comfortable existence

11

hedges, built attractive houses and villages out of the natural stone, and nursed the land to make it both beautiful and productive. We haven't fought over our countryside much, and we have stopped other people from doing so, thus preventing the destruction of much of our old building. We have admittedly changed its face quite dramatically at times, especially by enclosing the open fields but, however morally unjustifiable that may have been when it was done, it is now aesthetically pleasing.

British people love their countryside and have created an enviable and tolerant way of life within it based around the farm, village or market town. It is a way of life that completely embraces the land and its wildlife, with complicated social structures and traditions that preserve the landscape. They have been generated over thousands of years. It is an arrogant generation which tampers with them.

Whereas in many societies it is the city which attracts people, with its easy living and cultural pleasures, our natural magnet is back to our countryside. The successful Dutchman built himself a town house and filled it with works of art; the Russian escaped from the boredom of his flat and featureless plain to the delights of St Petersburg or Moscow; the first priority of the residents of many Third World countries is to get a city life and to forget their rural roots which they regard as synonymous with hard work and poverty. We, by contrast, get a genuine pleasure from living in our countryside or visiting it if we can't live there, and the ambition of many successful Britons is still to make enough money

"We, by contrast, get a genuine pleasure from living in our countryside or visiting it if we can't live there"

to retire to it. There have been exceptions: "I nauseate walking," wrote Congreve in *The Way of the World*, " 'tis a country diversion, I loathe the country", but generally there is a Pan in most of us, even though we are now predominantly a suburban society, and his pipes play through the layers of sophistication with which we surround ourselves.

The travel writer Freya Stark, who visited much of this world and knew intimately many of its different landscapes and societies, wrote, "I have often wondered what catches us so sharply in the landscapes of Asia. They are hardly ever as beautiful as ours. There is no Afghan plain that I have seen as lovely as the Thames Valley from Cliveden Woods." There are, of course, beautiful landscapes the world over, but there is something very special about our British countryside and it is not only British people who find it so. Drive along a British motorway, or even better make a journey by train, and you will see out of your window an endlessly changing pattern of colour, shape and form. It is a confidential landscape for the most part, and nothing is obvious. The pleasure lies in wondering what is beyond the wood on the hill or what sort of house hides behind that wall. What is that village with an impossibly complicated name to which you have just seen a signpost really like? Our pleasure is in both the natural beauty and the rural society we have built within it. Compare this with a drive through many European countries, where, however beautiful the landscape, the fields are open and wide, the villages easily seen and compact, the woods larger and the view to the horizon unambiguous.

The pleasure also lies in the contrast. We have a staggering variety of landscape packed into a very small space but it's not just the contrast between hill and plain or marsh and down. It is the contrast in the seasons, in agriculture, in types of building, in the birds and the wildflowers and trees. It's driving from a Cornish fishing village with seagulls chattering over the gorse-covered cliffs to the bleak granite of Bodmin Moor with its remote farms on an autumn afternoon; or watching a fox steal across a ride in a

southern English woodland in the still of a winter's morning with icy cobwebs hanging on the bare trees and returning to the same spot in the spring to find the bluebells out and green shoots everywhere. It's in watching combine harvesters on a summer evening under a wide sky on an English down and then dropping into the valley of a chalk stream as the cows come in to milk. It's listening to partridges calling, or the distant chiming of a church bell in a Cotswold meadow; it's seeing the late summer sunlight fall on a Welsh hillside as the sheep graze, or the autumn sea break on the harbour wall of a Northumbrian fishing village set around with grey cottages; it's waking up to a fall of fresh snow on a winter's morning in Aberdeenshire, or watching the dirty power of a Highland river in spate.

The British have not made a success of living in towns, despite the fact that we are now largely an urban and suburban society. We are not natural town dwellers as we need space around us, and our priority in cities is to develop parks or allotments that remind us of the country that our grandfathers left so recently during the Industrial Revolution. Sociologists can fantasise as only they know how, but ultimately they must accept that British man has always been bred as a country animal and that it will take him half a millennium to adjust to the crowded life of the city. This makes it even more important to preserve our unique and beautiful countryside with its way of life that has given us our national character, and to preserve it as the living countryside it has always been – not the sterile museum some would have it become. We are part of the countryside in which our ancestors lived and by which they and subsequently we were conditioned; it is also part of us. If we do not realise its true value, we will have lost our national identity.

The greatest threat to our British countryside is that the majority of our population do not understand it

The Countryside Under Threat

Robin Hanbury-Tenison

The South American rainforest is one of the richest habitats on earth. Its tribal people are its best guardians. The threat to their environment and lifestyle is, correctly, the object of international campaigns; campaigns in which I have been at the forefront most of my life. It is ironic that here in Britain we also have a unique environment but there is no international movement to save us! Yet our countryside and its special way of life is as much under threat as the South American Indians in their rainforest. We are in danger of squandering our greatest inheritance, the envy of every other country in the world. No finer-managed landscape exists anywhere and it is maintained in its delicate equilibrium by the people who live and work in it.

The extent to which man has influenced the fauna and flora of the planet is only now being recognised, and nowhere is this truer than in Europe. Here, constant culling and deforestation followed by replanting and re-introductions of extinct or alien species has created one of the most artificial landscapes on earth. In parts of Europe, misuse and over-exploitation have brought about situations where the ecosystems are barren and close to collapse, but in Britain we still have the richest and most dynamic countryside. Much of the credit for this must go to those who work and maintain it and those who come to take part in the activities which sustain it. For example, by developing humane and

sustainable codes of practice, all field sports today contribute to the enhancement of the countryside, while at the same time providing employment and pleasure to millions.

"The problem is that we now expect our countryside to be frozen in time"

The greatest threat to our British countryside and the way of life it supports is that the majority of our population do not understand it. We have become a nation of city and suburb dwellers, sanitised from nature, who have lost touch with the real countryside. 89% of our population are urban dwellers (we have the ninth-highest urban population density in the world) and only 11% are countrymen. Only 1.7% of our Gross Domestic Product is derived from agriculture (and we also rank ninth in the world of those countries least dependent on agriculture). A mere 10% of the United Kingdom is covered by woodland, the lowest figure for any European country except for Holland and Ireland. 27% of France is still forested, 30% of Germany and 67% of Japan.

We certainly still like our countryside, and many of us want to move back out of our towns and suburbs to live in it. The rural vote is considerably higher than the number of people who work in rural jobs. The problem is that we want the countryside to conform to the image that we have developed of how it should be. This image is of the perfect village, with thatched cottages set about a duck pond, surrounded by woods and meadows full of flowers. This 'chocolate box' vision of rural England may be a bit wide of the mark but it is an aspiration, and much of our enviable countryside lends itself to being so idealised. The problem is that we now expect our countryside to be frozen in time. We want the ideal perpetuated but fail to understand the forces that created

it in the first place. Rural society and the countryside economy are under threat from those who do not understand that for their ideal to survive it must support those who live in it and conserve it. People must be able to get jobs, to afford houses, to educate their children, to farm the land and to continue country practices without being persecuted by those who do not understand their lifestyle. If you kill the countryside and replace it with a vast National Park, Britain will soon look and feel like a very different country.

Single issue pressure groups exploit this lack of understanding of the countryside to their own ends. Whether they are opposed to farming practices, to field sports or to roads, they work on the basis that the majority will support their protest because they have no knowledge of the alternative. They are as pernicious as those logging companies who are destroying the rainforest. Field sports are a perfect example of single issue politics at work; as Chief Executive of The British Field Sports Society, I have a vested interest in exposing the fallacy of the anti-field sports lobbyists. They never tell you that foxes have to be controlled and that if they weren't hunted they would die more painful deaths because they are preaching to a population who do not know anything about foxes. One sometimes suspects that they might be deriving their knowledge of how animals behave from watching *The Animals of*

"by developing humane and sustainable codes of practice, all field sports today contribute to the enhancement of the countryside"

Farthing Wood. Perhaps the supreme irony came when John McFall, the MP who introduced the anti-hunting bill into Parliament last spring, admitted on *Newsnight* that he had never been hunting but only seen a hunt on video. I have no argument with those who really do know about hunting but who still choose to oppose it. That is their right. But equally such people tend to respect the right of those people who do hunt to continue to do so.

Animal rights is not a movement underpinned by sound ethical or conservation principles; it is an extremist campaign that absurdly places the survival of the individual animal over that of the species and which trades on the average Briton's ignorance of the ways of the countryside. A natural successor to the student protests of the sixties and the anti-Vietnam and ban the bomb movements of the seventies, it has cleverly harnessed environmentalism to its own ends. According to its founder, the Australian Peter Singer, "Once you are against the military/industrial complex in general, well, it doesn't take much to see its effect on the environment and the rest of the world". Of course, another irony is that all South American Indians hunt!

Field sports are but one of many issues where pressure groups affect the countryside adversely and political parties draft policies based on what they think people want rather than on what is actually beneficial. Nor have politicians done much for the rural economy in recent years. One of the greatest challenges facing the young in the rural community is getting a job. Agriculture employs fewer and fewer people as farming

technology improves and it does not pay well. Fewer farms now offer housing and the increase in weekenders and the holiday cottage business means that house prices are high. Supermarkets on the edge of towns, and weekenders not shopping locally, mean that fewer villages have economically viable shops and many do not have the transport services to take people into towns. Social facilities are scarce; local authorities centralise schools in towns; and the police seem unable to maintain village bobbies. All this means that the

young tend to move away, leaving the countryside to the retired or the casual resident. Ironically, those moving to the countryside from the towns because they aspire to the life it offers are unwittingly changing the character of that life for the worse.

They also have time to serve on local bodies and it is increasingly the newcomer who quickly comes to represent the local community. This social mobility is one of the strengths of British society. People are now reversing the migration their great-grandparents made at the time of the Industrial Revolution a century ago. But urban emigrants should not pander to their own whims at the expense of the community as a whole; planning controls are beneficial but only if sensibly applied; bans on hunting on council land are often not supported by a majority of those who pay council tax. One man's rural idyll is another man's unemployment.

One of the greatest influences on the countryside has been the increase in car ownership. Cars work both ways in rural society. They allow people living in the countryside to travel to use the facilities of the local

towns and to run businesses from more remote locations, but cars also allow more and more people to travel out of towns to enjoy the countryside. Nothing wrong in that, and the money they spend on leisure activities keeps many rural industries going. Yet the number of people visiting the countryside does cause problems. Freedom of access is becoming a debated subject. No one wants to prevent their urban neighbour from sharing in the countryside's beauty but if too many people share it then the beauty will disappear – crumbled under the thousands of feet that destroy the footpaths in the Fells, or scared away by the ramblers who disturb the peace of nesting birds.

A balance has to be struck between access and conservation. Were every visitor to the countryside educated in its ways at school, then the problem would be easier to solve. Sadly, too many of our population are epitomised by the schoolteacher visiting a farm in Derbyshire who told her charges that the milk they drank came from bottles and that it was unkind to take it from a cow.

Farmers, and modern farming practice, are themselves part of the problem. A farmer is in a unique and sometimes rather unenviable position in today's society. He is responsible for a huge area of the nation (74% of our total land area in 1994 compared to 16% in urban or industrial use) yet his returns are small. He has been a victim of rapidly changing government policies, many of which are decided by authorities in Brussels over whom he has little control. When he behaves like a businessman and tries to maximise his profit he is accused of being uncaring and raping the landscape, whilst if he retains traditional practices he tends to go bust. Currently, times are good for some but they can change very quickly. Society correctly expects farmers to conserve the character of our countryside but, if they are to do so, they must enjoy stable conditions.

Much work has been done to reduce pollution but a residual threat remains. Chemicals have been responsible for the disappearance of much of our wildlife. We must try to make farming as ecologically sound as possible whilst not insisting that it becomes uneconomic. Similarly, we need to watch the pollution of our rivers, whether from industrial waste or agricultural effluent.

Lastly, the division in the ranks of those organisations who defend the countryside is a threat in itself. There are too many bodies pursuing individual agendas without regard to the whole. You cannot logically separate any one element of the countryside and argue its cause in isolation. The rural economy and society, farming, field sports and conservation are all constituent part of one body. Together the countryside can muster many millions of votes (five million for field sports alone). These must not be wasted.

The British countryside and its way of life are unique. They have given us our national character. They must be preserved as a living

entity. We need to compare the proud record of environmental management of the countryside with the tragedy of urban decay. Sometimes we are apologists for our way of life – we must not be. The rural way of life is healthy, respected and sound. It must be defended against the threats that I have outlined. We must also respect its antiquity and realise that we cannot let the antics of a single misinformed generation jeopardise our inheritance. That lack of understanding, which I have emphasised, must be replaced with knowledge, and that will only come through education. There is a need to explain how the countryside is run; to show how man has intervened sympathetically and successfully with nature and how the balance of the countryside can be maintained. In the following chapters the themes that I have introduced are developed in more detail.

Robin Hanbury-Tenison is an explorer, conservationist, author and farmer. Named by The Sunday Times *as "the greatest explorer of the past 20 years", he has been on 24 major expeditions and has been awarded the Gold Medal of the Royal Geographical Society. His research in Sarawak and Borneo started the international concern for tropical rainforests. He was one of the founders of Survival International, the worldwide movement to support tribal peoples and is now its President. Nearer home he is a Trustee of the Ecological Foundation, a Patron of the National Forum Trust, was President of the Cornwall Wildlife Trust for eight years and is now Chief Executive of the British Field Sports Society.*

"Society correctly expects farmers to conserve the character of our countryside but, if they are to do so, they must enjoy stable conditions"

Fishing
John Wilson

*O*urs is indeed a strange attitude. Within our industrialised Western society, the city dweller is perfectly content to purchase from the local supermarket a piece of frozen, headless fish or meat wrapped in clingfilm, not knowing or even caring from which particular creature it came. It obviously had to be killed by someone, yet that same city dweller will subsequently condemn the countryman who shoots a rabbit for his dinner, or who fishes for sport. So, until the men in white coats come for me, I shall continue to hunt where and when the fancy takes me and to fish until I drop.

I guess it is the sheer mystery of it all that continues to capture my imagination after half a century of peering into the depths of water, when and wherever I happen to be in the wild. And I often think I could even fish happily in a bucket of water providing the bottom couldn't be seen, and there was just half a chance of the float tip bobbing under.

I care not whether the day is swelteringly hot or miserably cold; whether it is blowing a gale or deathly still in the grip of winter. Indeed, with the lake frozen over and crystallised hoar-frost covering waterside shrubbery, there is no finer moment for removing the lens cap from my camera and leaving the rods in the car. Many is the time when half a day spent fishing has included not a single cast. Yet I have returned home completely satisfied.

"Why Mother Nature made man a hunter or apples for picking is for no one on this earth to question"

Even when river margins are frozen over there is such marvellous magic to see. Raw certainly, but beautiful nonetheless. Simply being there, walking along whilst observing the river's flow patterns without so much as making a single cast, is commitment enough. For there will be other times when such information can be put to good use. It is perhaps as close as the fisherman can ever come to the experiences and feeling of his ancestors who, regardless of weather conditions, fished purely to survive. And this very same inner feeling is something all fishermen treasure, yet find difficult to explain to our families and friends, who sit at home in comfortable warmth, content in the belief that we all must indeed be certifiable.

"I guess it is the sheer mystery of it all that continues to capture my imagination after half a century of peering into the depths of water"

To ardent anglers such as I, few moments in time can match that boyish excitement of rising at dawn on a summer's morning with birds in full chorus and clouds of grey mist hugging the river bank. The chill, the unknown quantity, the smell of crushed water mint, the sight of dew-covered spiders' webs hanging from marginal grasses and the disapproving 'honk' of an old heron as he indignantly takes off – the greatest and quietest fisherman of them all. Bubbles erupting on the surface from deep down suggest fish are feeding earnestly. But is the water too clear? Will they fancy the flavour of paste carefully prepared the evening before?

From nowhere a kingfisher zooms low along the river like a bolt of cobalt blue lightning, *en route* from one perch to another. He also has a family to feed.

The float tip lifts slowly and a firm strike connects with unseen power. The forearm supporting the rod is jagged down and the sense of mystery which has curdled in my brain since I first wore short trousers is instantly switched on. Is it one of those huge bream I've seen but never managed to hook, or is it merely an aggressively powerful male tench? For a second I ponder, and question the coincidence that Mother Nature should supply such aggression to the males of her species, but that split second of lost concentration costs me dearly. The monster has alas managed to transfer my hook into a long sprig of hornwort, a crunchy water weed which in certain environments takes on a smell of the sea.

I am totally deflated for several seconds. A new piece of paste is pressed on the hook. Bubbles are thankfully still bursting into the oily surface film despite the commotion of losing a fish. My enthusiasm is instantly renewed and expectation levels are reaching to the point of climax.

There is no conclusion to a fishing tale. Go fishing and experience it for yourself, and do, please, see fishing in its proper perspective, as do the odd three million sport fishermen in Britain who you will be joining.

Why Mother Nature made man a hunter or apples for picking is for no one on this earth to

question. For it will always be a dog eat dog and a fish eat fish world in which over-populations of certain species have been well catered for by our creator.

Can you imagine, for instance, if reptiles, amphibians, fish, spiders, bats and birds did not catch and consume the largest proportion of hatched insects both terrestrial and water-borne? The insects would reproduce ten-fold in as many days and the world as we know it could simply not survive.

We are all part of an intricate global ecosystem which constantly changes (remember the dinosaurs?) whether we like it or not, which is why man should never relinquish his basic instinct for hunting. People who preach vegetarianism, anti this and anti that, tend not to understand what they are talking about and wouldn't recognise a viviparous lizard from a toadstool if they sat on one.

I am a hunter first and foremost, proud of it, and I have been put on this earth as such. It is why I go fishing. It is, in fact, a need in me and something I could not quash even if I wanted to, any more than I could stem the urge felt throughout adult life for propagation of my species. They are physical characteristics handed down by my ancestors. I also fish for pleasure because it satisfies all those animal instincts in which we need fulfilment. I do occasionally fish for food, specifically to feed myself or others, though generally I am content to take enjoyment from watching an adversary swim away, to fight another day. And here perhaps lies the sporting element in man.

I cannot alter how I feel towards the sports of hunting, shooting and fishing any more than the domesticated dog which sleeps indoors and walks on Axminster carpet can stop itself from walking around in a circle (as it does in the wild to flatten grass) before slumping down into sleeping mode beside the fire.

That one saying, that "you can take the animal out of the jungle, but not the jungle out of the animal" is so perfectly true – even in the case of man. For you can take man away from the hunt but not his instincts for hunting. Those who try are now paying the price.

A great sadness of our contemporary inner city life is the way in which children now grow up in high-rise flats without gardens or access to wild places and thus have their basic curiosity towards a love of natural history greatly suppressed. Sadly, when their hunting instincts do develop, as they surely will, without water, land and trees to climb and without wild places and animals upon which to vent their pent-up natural aggression, they take it out on, and even hunt, fellow human beings.

I would wager all that I own on the belief that aggravated crime in the UK is per headcount far lower in the countryside where teenagers can go hunting, shooting or fishing, than in the streets of an urban concrete jungle where lager-lout hooligans track down the old and infirm for an easy kill.

In truth there are times when, due to my total involvement with fishing which includes fisheries management, writing and producing programmes for television, I become totally irritated by continually having to substantiate my love of the sport. After all, I have never seen fit during *my* weekend off to spend the entire time ensuring that others do not enjoy themselves.

John Wilson is known to millions as TV's Mr Angling, having presented over 60 Go Fishing *programmes for Anglia, Channel Four and Meridian Television. Fishing has taken John all round the globe and he is recognised as one of the world's greatest anglers.*

He has run a tackle shop in Norwich for 25 years. Living west of the city in a lakeland setting, John concentrates on fisheries management when not filming or writing.

Author of more than 20 books, and contributing chapters to a further 30, John writes regularly for The Angling Times *and various glossy monthlies.*

"A great sadness of our contemporary inner city life is the way in which children now grow up… without… access to wild places"

Shooting
Jack Charlton

I fired my first shot with a shotgun when I was about 12 or 13 – I forget which exactly. We were flighting duck off the shore at Newbiggin onto a pond just inland. My father taught me to shoot. He was a miner and a great countryman. His hobbies were whippets, keeping pigs, gardening and shooting. I went away soon after that to play football and didn't pick up a gun again until I was 25 or 26. I had started to play golf but got fed up with it, not that golf is a bad game, it was just I couldn't get the hang of it. One day I threw my clubs in a river and went back to shooting. I used to shoot with a few friends in those days, including Jeff Gunny, the great rugby player. It was rough shooting and we would walk for miles for not very much, except the odd pigeon, but it was great fun.

I've shot ever since. But not in Ireland. I didn't have much time although I was asked to shoot snipe and woodcock. Also you had to be a bit careful coming backwards and forwards with guns because of the troubles. Once I was stopped going onto the Stranraer ferry with a big bag of cartridges on the back seat and no shotgun certificate with me, but luckily the police recognised me and looked after them until I got back.

The greatest fun I've had recently was on a moor a few of us rented in Yorkshire. It wasn't big – only about 400 acres which is small for a grouse moor – but it was very prolific. It was on the edge of a much bigger moor and had a lot of water. Eight of us ran it together; eight lads going up and working it for each other. We didn't use pointers, just

"…the camaraderie of being out and about in the countryside together"

normal shooting dogs. Two or three of us would drive and the others stand. It wasn't expensive. Our group were mostly working lads from Leeds – but it was really special having your own place like that. Sadly we lost it last year. Now we have a bit of rough shooting near Middlesbrough where we put down a few birds. It's not driven – it really is rough but great to walk round with a few lads. And I get asked to quite a lot of organised invitation shoots these days. I enjoy them. They're very difficult but a great challenge – although there is one I've been to a couple of times in Wales where the birds are so high they make a mockery of you.

People often ask me why I enjoy shooting. There are lots of reasons. There is so much to it. First, I'm meeting my friends, and especially people I don't see often. Then there is the camaraderie of being out and about in the countryside together, working for each other and seeing your dogs work. Thirdly, there is the pleasure of being in the countryside itself and relaxing after all those football matches and dinners. Then I get asked how I can kill something. People say "How do you feel?" and I say, "Much the same as when my father told me when I was a boy to go out to the yard and wring a chicken's neck for Sunday lunch." It's extraordinary how illogical people can be. They're quite happy to eat meat and fish but they think it's wrong to kill animals.

People are "quite happy to eat meat and fish but they think it's wrong to kill animals"

People also don't realise just how much shooting does
for the countryside. There are those, townspeople
mainly, who don't realise that without shooting there
wouldn't be any game birds. The countryside can't
look after itself. It's got to be policed. Once you stop
shooting, the wildlife disappears. I had a real row with
a politician in Sheffield once. There was a lovely
wooded area near the town that belonged to the
Council. It was a lovely place, where three valleys met

and it should have been full of wildlife. Then I walked round it one day
and didn't see a living thing, apart from one hare and some rooks and
crows. I discovered that the Council had banned shooting up there so
no one had bothered to look after it. I took this politician up on it and
said, "Look, this is what happens when you ban shooting!"

Without shooting there would be far fewer woods. If it hadn't been
for all those with a bit of land who enjoyed shooting – and foxhunting
– there would be no coverts. Farmers wouldn't bother to keep coverts
if they got no benefit from them. Then there are keepers feeding birds
all winter – and all sorts of wildlife benefit from that. There was a big
estate next to me when I lived at Barnsley and it wasn't shot. I used to
see people going past with dogs and lamps – it was near a mining area,
and some miners are funny lads. They think they've got a God-given
right to go anywhere. And that estate was dead – poached to hell
because it wasn't keepered. Shooting polices the countryside in a way
that nothing else can.

*"People also don't realise
just how much shooting
does for the countryside"*

Shooting is my great pleasure in life. Football is wonderful but it's work. Shooting is my relaxation. There is nothing to beat being out in the British countryside with your friends and your dogs. It would be a very silly government who misread the British people so badly that they tried to take away our pleasure.

Jack, a miner's son from Ashington, won every distinction in English football and a World Cup winners medal in 1966. As a manager his unprecedented success with the Republic of Ireland established him as one of the world's best known honorary Irishmen. Throughout his glittering career in professional sport he has always sought relaxation in the countryside, equally at home with gun and rod.

Riding

Michael Clayton

Despite all that the twentieth century has wrought on the British countryside it remains one of the world's best environments for horse riding.

Many of those who like riding, and jumping hedges and timber at speed across grass would assert firmly that Britain is still *the* best. It is the challenge of crossing country that has shaped equestrianism in our small island, and it remains a powerful influence even though additional new horse sports have evolved in this century to accompany our living traditions of hunting and racing. Horses and mules remained a vital part of military transport in both world wars. The Second World War speeded up the displacement of the horse as a means of transport and greatly increased the use of machinery in farming.

Yet at the end of the twentieth century some three million Britons ride horses and ponies with widely varying levels of skill and frequency, and in an ever-widening range of sports. Our horse and pony population is about half a million, more than the early post-war years when breeding levels had dropped generally, and the heavy horse suffered especially through the greater use of lorries, vans and tractors. Our love of horses for recreation and sport has caused a surge in horse and pony breeding since the 1960s.

After the Second World War, the Turf and the Chase remained the twin pillars of British riding, and military traditions and influence were crucial.

"Our love of horses for recreation and sport has caused a surge in horse and pony breeding since the 1960s"

This was allied with a powerful tradition of cross-country riding among the farming community, plus a significant number of professional and business people who hunted regularly. The needs of generations of sporting riders had been met by the development of the jewel in the British equestrian crown, the Thoroughbred horse – and the existence of no less than nine breeds of native ponies on which our children could first experience the thrills, and the perils, of life in the saddle.

The Cavalry's own riding academy at Weedon in Northamptonshire had been largely responsible for teaching the art and science of equitation in England until it was closed in 1940 – and alas, it did not re-open after the war, unlike the French Cavalry school at Saumur, home of the Cadre Noir corps of instructors, who from 1969 supervised tuition at the nearby National School of Equitation. In Britain, Cavalry officers trained in pre-war years at Weedon played a major role in reorganising our sports.

The extraordinary speed of post-war expansion was due largely to the survival, in limited form, during the war of hunting and racing. The framework of sport in the countryside remained intact, and it was gratefully filled by men and women returning from all forms of war service. No one was more influential than the late Colonel Sir Mike Ansell, who returned blinded from a German prisoner-of-war camp and set about reviving

and rebuilding the sport he had enjoyed so much before the war: show jumping. He gave the sport a huge impetus, and with Dorian Williams as an inspired TV commentator, it put equestrianism for the first time on millions of British screens, giving a major boost to riding as a sport and attracting many recruits. Colonel Sir Harry Llewellyn's round on his horse Foxhunter in Britain's gold medal winning team at the Helsinki Olympic Games in 1952 became a legend of horsemanship which inspired many to take up riding for the first time. Colonel Mike's creation, the Horse of the Year Show, and the revived Royal International Horse Show, added hugely to the prestige of riding as a pastime for millions.

Yet no more influential lead could have been given than that of our Royal Family. They are steeped in equestrianism in many spheres, and have given patronage and encouragement springing from centuries of royal involvement in racing and hunting.

The Queen's love of flat racing, and her involvement in bloodstock breeding, follows a childhood when she was encouraged to ride by King George VI and Queen Elizabeth, both passionately fond of horses. There has been no more popular owner and patron of National Hunt racing than the Queen Mother, and the late King was a keen hunting man in the Shires.

The Queen's interest extends to most areas of the horse world, and one of her lesser known successes was the breeding of top-class polo ponies for the Prince of Wales. His discovery of the hunting field began in his

twenties, and nowadays he is a highly competent rider across country and has hunted with over 40 packs. He has said that visiting Hunts proved to be a wonderful way of exploring the British countryside on a horse, and meeting many country people. Much of England, especially the famous Midlands hunting countries, had been a sea of grass between the wars. Huge wartime increases in arable farming, and post-war farming policies, meant that many acres of rideable old turf went under the plough for the first time for many generations.

The motorway network started in the 1960s, and an annual loss of farmland to building and other development began to surge ahead. Hunting people noted the changes with apprehension long before it became a popular 'green' issue. "This will kill hunting," predicted the pessimists, as they had done when railways and canals appeared in the previous century.

A more vocal anti-hunting movement appeared among the urban-based, although the first Parliamentary attempt to ban the sport was soundly defeated in the House of Commons in 1949.

Far from shrinking, riding to hounds increased remarkably during the post-war years.

The most important influence in maintaining a culture of horsemanship in the countryside has been the Pony Club, founded in 1929, wisely linking most branches firmly with the Hunts.

Thus generations of children have had the chance to maintain proper standards of horsemanship, including horse care, with the opportunity presented at a very early age to relish the hunting field as natural playground.

They learned to ride in all weathers, to save their ponies during a long winter's day in the saddle, to jump all kinds of obstacles off varied surfaces, and to observe the discipline of the hunting field which is essential in looking after the interests of hunting's hosts, the landowners and farmers. Best of all, the Pony Club encourages the vital precept expressed by Surtees through his great creation, the Cockney hunting grocer, John Jorrocks: "Happy is he who goes out to please himself and not to astonish others." This does not mean, however, that competitive riding has not been part of the Pony Club tradition. It has played a huge role in developing Britain as a highly successful international riding nation, but the Pony Club today still insists that all-round horsemanship, including the care of the pony, is more important than winning trophies and prize money. It has nearly 40 000 members in 368 branches throughout the United Kingdom and it has been copied widely abroad.

The British tradition of cross-country riding was closely linked to the development of riding over fences which followed the enclosure of land in the late eighteenth and early nineteenth centuries with cut and laid hedges, and timber rails. Previously, small obstacles and ditches were usually jumped from a virtual standstill. A Shropshire squire named Mr

Childe, known as 'Flying Childe', introduced to Leicestershire his own art of flying fences at a gallop. The 'oxer', still seen in show jumping fence design, was a timber guard rail in front of a hedge to prevent oxen maddened by summer flies from breaking through. It became a formidable extra element in clearing a hedge, often lined with an open ditch as well.

Such challenges called for horses of quality and courage, and from the late eighteenth century they were used for racing as well as hunting.

Riding from 'point-to-point' derives from the old practice of hunting men racing each other across country from the point of one church spire to the next; hence steeple chasing was the name given to the sport when, in the nineteenth century, such races were run over more or less marked-out courses.

Racing over fences in Britain and Ireland is one of the great glories of our sporting scene. Point-to-pointing, amateur racing over fences for negligible prize money, takes place from January to May, and is run by the Hunts, using voluntary officials on widely varying courses. The sport has never been more popular; there were 203 fixtures in the 1996 season, involving about 13 000 runners.

Racing over fences or hurdles, under Jockey Club Rules on permanent courses, has its great festivals in Cheltenham and Aintree, but is popular on many lesser courses, and is nowadays nearly a 12 months' sport. As the distinguished Newmarket trainer Tom Jones pointed out in his 1995 Gimcrack speech, the connections between racing and the hunting field remain vital.

Many owners had their interest in jump racing fired by their own riding experiences in the hunting field and in point-to-pointing and hunter 'chasing', the next rung up the amateur riding ladder.

Britain's cross-country tradition was a major factor in our brilliant series of post-war successes at top international levels in the sport of horse trials. Again, royal example helped to encourage many recruits. The Princess Royal's win on her horse Doublet in the European Championships in 1971 at Burghley, and her many other successes, greatly increased media interest, but the great British three-day-events at Badminton and Burghley continue to attract huge attendances of spectators in spring and autumn. The original inspiration for the founding of both Badminton and Burghley came from landowning Masters of Foxhounds, the 10th Duke of Beaufort and the Marquess of Exeter respectively.

Since the war, Britain has won at the Olympic Games three gold and two silver team medals in horse trials, and a team gold, silver and bronze medal in show jumping.

Our successes at this level have helped to encourage large-scale British sponsorships for all kinds of equestrianism at home. Perhaps because of our cross-country riding traditions, dressage was a slower starter in gaining wider British support in the post-war years, but it

is now one of the fastest growing specialist disciplines, and although Germany continues to dominate much of the international sport, British standards are rising considerably at all levels.

The Duke of Edinburgh was one of the prime movers in the development of competition carriage driving, writing rules for the sport, and participating as an expert in driving four-in-hand, pairs and singles. He had given polo a great post-war boost at Windsor, and active encouragement of the game at junior level by the Pony Club has been a major factor in this sport's post-war growth.

The Pony Club also organises polo-cross with much success and it has long held national competitions in gymkhana games, culminating in the annual contests at the Horse of the Year Show. Britain's team victory in Endurance Riding at the Stockholm World Championships in 1990 gave a great boost to that comparatively new sport in this country. Vaulting is another sport which has growing participation.

In the cross-country area, traditional hunter trials are still popular, but in 1974 Douglas Bunn invented team chasing at Hickstead, and it has survived as a thrilling sport at open and novice levels all over Britain, with teams of four competing over cross-country courses against the clock.

The diversity and specialisation of British riding has produced headaches for organisers, and huge problems

for organised horse and pony breeding. Thoroughbred breeding, thanks to its commercial basis as the provider of young horses for the flat and jump racing, remains highly successful, and a major earner overseas.

Leading Arab owners came to Britain, despite our lesser prize money compared with many other racing nations, because the diversity of our courses, the framing of our Classic season, and the high standards of breeding, continue to give our Turf unique advantages.

American and other overseas hunting men and women continue to enjoy the thrills of riding over grass and fences in our Shires hunting fields in the East Midlands, and the wildness of hunting on our beautiful, unspoilt moorlands, such as Exmoor and Dartmoor. New Zealanders, and other overseas riders, base their horses in Britain to enjoy our extraordinarily varied and full horse trials season.

The All England Jumping Course at Hickstead continues to attract some of the world's best showjumpers to Douglas Bunn's creation of a permanent jumping course. Our country shows circuit, and Royal Windsor Horse Show – the largest outdoor show in Britain – provide a marvellous shop window for in-hand young stock and ridden horses in a huge variety of showing classes. So much activity and variety has placed huge strains on the structure of the British Horse Society (BHS), founded in 1947. Not only does it run all the principal equestrian sports outside racing (except for showjumping which has its own organisation), the BHS also has the vital tasks of battling for bridleway rights, setting standards in riding qualifications, training, welfare and safety, especially on modern roads which are increasingly dangerous for the horse and pony.

In 1996, the structure of the BHS and the British Equestrian Federation, which represents this country on the international scene, was being closely examined by a high-level working party, with a view to reforming the entire organisation to meet the challenges of the twenty-first century.

At the same time, major efforts were being made to encourage British competition horse and pony breeders to support a new database recording system, so that British stock could be better documented and selected, enabling it to compete more effectively with the much improved riding horses nowadays produced on the European continent, especially in Germany, Holland and France.

For the rider who simply wants to hack about the British countryside, the work of the BHS in fighting for bridleway rights is a vital reason for joining that organisation.

Alas, the fragmentation of British riding is a weakness in dealing with local and national government, although it is a strength in producing so many specialist centres of excellence.

The major fear of many British horsemen at the end of the century is that threats of legislation against hunting with hounds could one day succeed, thereby removing the working role of well over 50 000 horses and ponies currently used in the hunting field. Although some growth in drag-hunting would occur, it could not possibly cater for all those horses.

The hunting field's value as a training ground for young horses, or as a retirement role for older ex-competition horses would also be lost.

And there are grave fears that the loss of much of the British hunting field's access for mounted followers of foxhounds and harriers would gravely damage our great traditions in the art and skill of cross-country riding. Animal rights is an area where British horsemen are being drawn into conflict with misguided activists.

Some of the single issue fanatics have already indicated in words and in disruptive demonstrations that horse sports involving any form of risk to the horse are among their objectives for abolition.

It is hoped that wise politicians will be able to prevent Britain's equestrian traditions being irretrievably damaged or destroyed by a battle which is irrelevant to all that is best in riding in our still green and pleasant land.

Michael Clayton is the Editor-in-Chief of Horse & Hound, Country Life, The Field *and* The Shooting Times. *He was Editor of* Horse & Hound *from 1973-95, and is still a practical horseman, breeding and producing his own hunter stock in Leicestershire.*

Pony clubs encourage thousands of young children to learn about horses

Walking and Climbing

Chris Bonington

We are blessed to have in Britain some of the world's most wonderful country for walking and climbing. I have a very deep affection for our hills and mountains and I can describe best what they mean to me if I use, by way of example, the development of my own career as a climber.

It started peripherally! I was born in London just before the Second World War and sent off to a school in the south of the country, as an evacuee, at the tender age of five. After the collapse of France, the school was moved to the safety of Kirkby Lonsdale on the fringe of the Lake District. My grandmother used to come and spend the holidays with me in Grasmere and my great love of the Lake District really started then, but I did not feel an urge to climb until I was 16. I was staying with my maiden aunt in Wallasey and she had a book of black and white photographs of the Scottish Highlands. I was completely riveted. Soon afterwards I visited my grandfather who lived outside Dublin and whose house had a good view of the Wicklow Hills. I felt a desire to get up into them and walk there, which I duly did. On the way home I took the Dun Laoghaire to Holyhead ferry. The train from Holyhead passes to the north of Snowdonia and as I saw the great hills slip past I thought how wonderful it would be to explore the deep valleys and remote high tops.

Consequently, as soon as the next holidays came, I set off with a school friend just after Christmas to hitch-hike up the A5 to Snowdonia. Clad in snow, the mountains were as daunting to two young teenagers as

"the Lake District with all its memories of my wartime holidays"

the Himalayas. We climbed Moel Siabod and attempted Snowdon by the Pyg track but were avalanched off. My friend was put off for life and never looked at another mountain again but for me it just increased the excitement. I remember staying in a bed and breakfast after that experience and meeting there, for the first time in my life, some 'proper' climbers. I listened to them long into the night and realised that climbing was something I just had to try. Later that spring – it was 1951 – a friend took me to Harrison's Rocks, a small sandstone outcrop in Kent. I was completely hooked. I had found something that I was naturally good at and which enthralled me, as it has to this day.

I went to Wales in the Easter holiday, once again with a friend of the family, but he had to return home early because his children had mumps, leaving me to my own devices. I was sitting at the bottom of Idwal Slabs when a climber approached with two lads of my own age in tow. He looked like, and subsequently proved to be, a schoolmaster – Carl Verrinder. We fell into conversation and I joined his little team. I owe a lot to Carl. He realised that I had a natural ability and encouraged me to lead rather than follow as second on rope. That had a huge impact on me and in the next ten days I learned the basics of the craft. From then on my life was dominated by climbing and my schoolwork consequently suffered! I spent every summer camping in the Highlands, and walking and climbing our British hills has been part of my life ever since.

"she had a book of black and white photographs of the Scottish Highlands"

There is a quality to our hills which is very special. The great mountain ranges of the world are beautiful and incredibly exhilarating to explore but there is a depth to our British hills that makes them unique. It is the variety of tones of brown and green, the complexity of the shapes of ridge and valley, and the way that man in so many ways has left his influence; in the cropped grass of the high fells; the snaking dry stone walls and the farmhouses and cottages that nestle in the valleys as if rooted in the very ground.

There are two areas I would single out as having a very special place in my affections. The mountains of Wales, where I started my climbing and then spent two years as an instructor at the Army Outward Bound School at Towyn and, of course, the Lake District with all its memories of my wartime holidays. After leaving the Army I had a short interlude in London as a management trainee with Unilever, and got married to Wendy, but soon realised I needed a life built around my love of the mountains. It was my first British ascent of the North Wall of the Eiger that gave me the opportunity. I had something to write and lecture about. I could escape from London and had the delicious choice of being able to live anywhere I wanted. It was a toss-up between Snowdonia and the Lakes. The Lakes won. We started in a room above a farm in Ambleside, graduated to a furnished cottage in the Duddon Valley, then to one (unfurnished) in Ennerdale, bought a house in Cockermouth and then worked our way round to the north-east corner of the Lakes, above the village of Caldbeck, where we now live.

"There is a quality to our hills which is very special"

71

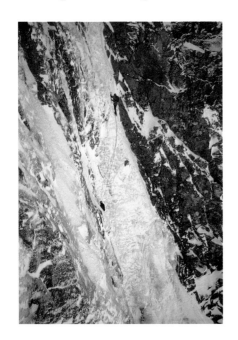

There is such an amazing variety in the Lake District, which on a world scale is tiny. It is a bit like a wheel, with the glaciated valleys being the spokes, stretching out from the centre, each one of them with its own special character. I have become particularly fond of the Northern Fells for they have a quality which separates them from the southern Lakes. The hills are more gentle and rolling and extraordinarily beautiful. Looking out from High Pike you can see north to the Solway Firth and the hills of Galloway, south to the main Lakes or east across the Eden Valley to the sweep of the Pennines.

Climbing is a process of self-discovery. I started with easy climbs and then worked my way up through the grades listed in the guide book on to harder and harder routes; began trying new lines that had never been touched before and through this discovered the joys of exploration. The next logical step is to go into the mountains in winter when they are covered in snow and ice. The Scottish Highlands give some of the best winter climbing in the world – scale is not everything. It is an evolutionary process that leads on to the greater peaks of the Alps, then the Himalayas. You learn to become attuned to the environment, not fighting it but becoming part of it, reading the weather, snow conditions and the lie of the land. This develops naturally into a greater awareness of our impact upon the environment and the need to keep this to the minimum, ideally leaving no trace of our presence.

On our own British hills this obviously means that we don't leave our rubbish behind, though sadly one still sees too many wrapping papers and bottles left on the summits of the most popular mountains. A more serious problem is the sheer number of people walking the hills. The outer fabric is threatened with destruction from the sheer volume of feet trampling the paths. The grass is worn away exposing the thin top soil. Running water compounds the damage, finding the foot-

made grooves, sculpting away even more of the earth and stones, and widening what started as a narrow runnel into a broad scar that defaces the entire hillside.

The use we make of the hills is more than just for recreation. It represents the chance of recharging batteries in lives that are increasingly pressured and technologically based. It is a form of therapy, inspiration and general uplift which is going to grow in importance as we move into the next century. Reducing the numbers of people going into the hills, quite apart from being difficult to implement, must never be seen as a solution. Our need for them is too great. The challenge, therefore, is to find ways of enabling people to venture into the hills without spoiling them.

The building of footpaths on routes affected by erosion is a sound practical solution. The type and quality of the path is very important. It would be regrettable to see the uplands defaced by concrete pathways – extensions of the roads that we are trying to escape. In the Lake District, particularly, a network of paths has been built using the available stone without the addition of concrete or other foreign materials, to enable people to enjoy the hills without destroying them.

I never tire of the Lake District. When coming back home from an expedition to one of the further ranges, from a lecture tour in this country or abroad, or just from a day in London, my heart always lifts as I approach the Howgill Gap, the dramatic valley bound by the outlying hills of the Lakes to the west and those of the Pennines to the east, where both the M6 and the railway are squeezed as the main link on the west coast between England and Scotland. For me, and I suspect many others, it is the gateway to the northern Lakes; a reminder that I am nearly home.

I revel in the walking that the Lakes provide. I go walking with my wife Wendy and our dog Bella, exploring out-of-the-way corners where, even on a Bank Holiday, when processions are marching up Scafell and Helvellyn, you can still escape the crowds at the end of the Duddon Valley, at the back of Ennerdale or on the rolling sweeps of the Northern Fells.

I love climbing in the Lakes as well. The cliffs are not huge by global standards. Even the crags of Scafell, the biggest in the Lake District, are only about 500 feet high. Once again there is a wonderful variety. Most of the mountain crags are igneous rocks, but on the edges are limestone, sandstone and slate, each having its own special character. I rarely go out for a complete day but slip out in the afternoon after doing a day's work at my writing and planning expeditions. I phone around until I find a fellow climber who is free, often meet him at the foot of the crag to snatch a climb or two before dusk, finishing off with a pint in one of the many superb Lakeland pubs.

I can still climb at around the same standard as when I was at the height of my powers in the 1960s and early 1970s, though, of course, the overall standard of climbing has gone rocketing up. At the age of 61 I have to accept that my time for hard climbing is finite, but even so I'm amazed that I can still climb to a reasonable standard and see no reason why I should not continue to do so for many more years. And when age does start taking its toll, I am sure that my joy in the hills will be undiminished even when the walks I can take amongst them might be very short and on the lower footpaths.

It makes my own commitment to the hills even greater to try to ensure that not only is access to our open fells preserved but that we care for the hills and crags in such a way that they remain unspoiled for future generations to enjoy.

Sir Christian Bonington CBE is the most famous British climber of his generation. He has led and been on 19 Himalayan expeditions, including four to Everest, which he climbed in 1985 at the age of 50, and has made many first ascents in the Alps and greater ranges of the world. His honorary appointments include President of the Alpine Club and President of the Council for National Parks. He has written 13 books and presented and appeared in many television programmes.

Wildlife
Robin Lowes

We are very lucky to live in a group of islands where position and climate give us a unique and beautiful countryside – and a marvellously varied wildlife to inhabit it. The contrast in our landscapes and our seasons is one of the great joys of the British countryside.

Winters come and winters go, and many seem extraordinarily reluctant to leave us. Drifts of snowdrops are still in full bloom as I write and it is already the third week of March!

Perhaps our long-range weather forecasters should take a course in ornithology – the most severe wintry weather we have experienced for years has brought ahead of it more fieldfares and redwings than I have seen in the south for some time. They arrived long before Christmas as if to warn us of the impending snows and frosts – last year we hardly saw a handful all winter.

In the Highlands it is a marvellous sight to see small parties of these birds flying in from their Icelandic and Norwegian summer haunts – rather like the first swallows in reverse – and, when out stalking in early October, witnessing the arrival of small parties of five or six, building up to massive numbers as the autumn days progressed. One particular day, leaving the glen below us, we travelled three miles along a hill road on one side of which hung a stunted wood of birch and rowan. Waves of fieldfares, mixed as so often with redwings, kept flying up ahead of us in their hundreds as they stripped the rowan berries from trees that a few days earlier had

looked like Christmas decorations. On our return in the afternoon there was hardly a bird to be seen, but that evening, and until most of the rowan berries in the surrounding hills had been devoured, the glen was moving with them, and each night they descended to the warmth of the larch and pine woods around the lodge where they had come to roost, their noisy chatter only subsiding when dark.

This winter has also brought considerable numbers of waxwings to our shores. Some years ago whilst working in London I telephoned a friend whose business was on the outskirts of Glasgow – from his office window he could just see the top of Ben Lomond covered in snow. He interrupted our conversation to say he had just seen a number of waxwings land on the edge of the guttering of the building opposite and help themselves to a drink. What a bonus to work with such a view! Waxwings are gregarious birds often moving around in quite large flocks, and when feeding on rowan berries, have the most endearing habit of picking and passing berries from one to another. An old superstition used to surround them, for it was thought that the appearance of these lovely birds was a portent of war or pestilence. I saw my first flock in 1941 but the war had already started! Legend has it that in days gone by, rowan were planted at the doors of Highland crofts and farm buildings to ward off evil spirits. Even now, when thinning out a wood behind the lodge, I was told by the contractor his men would not put an axe or saw to a rowan in case a broken arm, leg, or worse befell them shortly afterwards – and who was I to dispute it! Though rowan berries are bitter, they are often used to make jelly which

"leaving the glen below us, we travellled three miles along a hill road on one side of which hung a stunted wood of birch and rowan"

goes well with game or venison, and the sight of these trees in their highland home when set against the surrounding hills and rivers is quite spectacular.

After Christmas, snow fell over much of the country – we had less than our share in Sussex, but one night our automatic lights came on twice at the ungodly hour of 3 am. On each occasion I jumped out of bed to see what had caused it – easy enough I thought, for the ground was white with a two inch carpet of snow lit by a waning moon, but I had to wait until daylight to discover that our intruder had four legs and a bushy tail! The identity of our prowler would have been elementary even to Dr Watson, for a fox's tracks are unmistakable – his pad marks are placed one in front of the other so that the general effect is, unlike a dog, almost a straight line of footprints. In the wood, rabbit tracks were everywhere as if a whole army of them had been at work crossing and re-crossing each other, but a single rabbit will leave an awful number of prints behind him in a night.

Perhaps the most intriguing tracks were produced by a pair of otters walking side by side on an ice-covered river in the Scottish Highlands. A light powdering of snow had covered the ice, but the wind had blown much of it away, obliterating their usual tail marks in the process. The imprints of their pads, however, had frozen in remarkable clarity. Down-river their tracks had come together again as they journeyed on and, but for these on the snow-covered ice, we would never have known they were there.

Spring often comes late in the Highlands, but by mid-April the glen fills up with spring migrants, wheatears and meadow pipits being the first to arrive whilst winter migrants wing their way north.

One day in late April we were out on the hill at a height of about 1200 feet and stopped to watch two large skeins of geese flying fairly low as they followed a ridge for about a mile. It ended in a pronounced fork in the hills; to the left west, to the right north, and to the north they unhesitatingly swung. "That's the way I like to see them go," remarked the shepherd with us, and I knew just how much it must have meant to them all. That winter, with its short daylight hours, was behind them, despite what April, and even May, might still produce with their moods of sun, wind, rain and snow.

Myth and legend surround the fox as it does few other animals, often with an extraordinary cloak of sentimentality. That it is a creature of great beauty few will deny, but alas its killer instincts bring it into direct conflict with man. Sentimentality is often misplaced, but there is one delightful story of a friend who inadvertently allowed a very young terrier puppy to stray too near an earth containing fox cubs. The vixen rushed out of the bushes and knocked the pup over, probably fully intending to kill it, which she could easily have done in a second. But her maternal instincts would not let her do it; she realised that the pup was a baby, and instead of biting, she just held it down with her paws. As my friend shouted and ran, she made off

into the bushes again, turning to glance out once more before she disappeared. This bit of chivalry impressed him very much, and he resolved to be as fair as possible in his dealings with foxes in the future. Perhaps the expression 'innocent killers' would best fit, but it is an unfortunate fact that in the Highlands their numbers have increased ten-fold, due in large part to the sanctuary provided by the spread of forestry. John Colquhoun of *Moor and the Loch* fame had this to say about the hill fox: "The mountain fox is a splendid looking fellow, even the sneaking gait of the enemy of the poultry yard has in great measure left him; he seems to feel that he breathes a freer air, and lives by more noble plunder. He is extremely destructive to all game within his range and the havoc he makes among the hill lambs is a serious loss to the farmer." Written 130 years ago, it is just as true today.

In April another spring spectacular is underway. Many pools of water lying in boggy ground at heights up to 2000 feet will be the spawning arena for masses of frogs that gather there. Approach them too quickly or with heavy footsteps, and they will dive for cover. You will have quite a long wait for them to reappear, even if you keep very still. Sometimes their spawn is encrusted with ice, for in early April days, and especially nights, it can still be well below freezing at that altitude.

In April emperor moths appear too, the only British species of the silk-yielding *Saturnidae* family. These beautiful day-flying moths lay their eggs on the heather, on which their caterpillars feed, and they have a quite marvellous camouflage – rings of brown or purple spots circle their green bodies, depending on whether they are male or female. The caterpillars spin a brown cocoon in which they over-winter. This has an exit from which they eventually emerge, but through which no insect can enter, rather like an eel trap in reverse. Like many moths, the male can scent a female emperor moth by its feathery antennae up to half a mile away.

The majority of country dwellers hardly notice the enormous number and variety of moths living on their doorsteps. By and large, moths are nocturnal in habit – yet there are over 2000 species in Great Britain alone. Occasionally, an unusual one will fly through an open window after dark, drawn in by the light. More often than not it is considered an unwelcome guest, associated with such noxious visitors as cockchafers and other 'things that go bump in the night'.

A recent exception for us was a beautiful lime hawk moth that flew into the bedroom of a cottage we were staying in near the River Wye, and was found the next morning asleep on one of the curtains, remarkably similar in colour. I picked it up on the tip of my finger and put it outside on a wooden fence where it slept for the rest of the day.

Caterpillars are a different proposition. Nearly all garden plants, from roses to raspberries, provide food for one kind or another – woolly bears that turn into the strikingly colourful garden tiger moths; hawk moth caterpillars with their distinctive horned tails; or stick caterpillars, and many others that are known to most country folk. Unfortunately, many moths

are undoubted pests to farmers and gardeners, but I must confess I hate the thought of them being killed by those sprays used in the apple orchard.

Luckily, by no means all moths do harm whilst some, like woolly bears and the caterpillars of such butterflies as red admirals, peacocks, commas, and small tortoiseshells, cannot be faulted for choosing a nettlebed to feed on!

Recently when returning home by boat after fishing a Highland loch, my companion spotted a golden eagle gliding serenely along parallel to the ridge above us. Its serenity, however, was short-lived for at that precise moment, a peregrine falcon dived almost vertically at it like a bolt of blue, just as a spitfire might have once dived on a bomber, almost skiffing its back as it shot upwards to repeat the performance over and over again. Once or twice, the peregrine varied its tactics, making a much shallower approach at incredible speed from the rear before sailing upwards to revert to almost vertical dives in its efforts to drive the eagle away from what it must have considered its private domain. For all of five minutes we watched enthralled, for it almost seemed the peregrine's repeated attacks were being made for the sheer joy of flying.

"The countryside brings such rewards to the observant"

I cannot help recalling a recent farewell address at the funeral of a great friend, who had lived a marvellously full life, was a wonderful naturalist, and had

founded a gallery bringing artists together from the corners of the world to exhibit their paintings of all manner of natural life. The Rector recalled an art master setting his young class the most impossible task of painting God. One can imagine some of the efforts, but he came to one which depicted the most glorious landscape of river, trees and moorland. "That's a very beautiful painting," he said, "but where is God?" "Just look at the picture," came the reply, "God is everywhere."

The countryside brings such rewards to the observant and I feel deeply privileged to have had the chance to observe. Whether it be the icy clarity of winter and the familiarity of hungry birds, the renaissance of spring and hedgerow flowers; the thick scents of summer and the hum of insects, or the richness of autumn's fruits and the sounds of the rut, we have so much to enjoy.

After a distinguished naval career, Robin worked in industry. Despite this he has lived all his life in the country, either in Sussex or the Western Highlands of Scotland. He has a passion for the countryside and its wildlife and became a fishing fanatic at an early age. Robin is also a keen and experienced stalker. As an amateur photographer of note, his work has graced many magazine front covers.

"Just look at the picture," came the reply, "God is everywhere"

The Rural Economy
Michael Winter

The rural economy is in a state of transition arguably more profound than many earlier changes in the countryside. Indeed to find something at all similar we have to look back to the eighteenth and early nineteenth centuries when, under the impact of the Industrial Revolution, a mixed locally based economy was replaced by one dominated by commercial agriculture. The typical village community in, say 1750, was characterised by craftsmen and artisans producing for local markets with agriculture at the core as the primary industry. The economic base of the countryside became narrower as factory production in the towns took over from local craft-based manufacture. At a superficial level that process is now being reversed with agricultural employment declining and a more mixed and diverse rural economy emerging. Even in the remotest rural districts of England, agriculture accounts for little more than 6% of employment, and in many of the districts of shire counties it is as little as 3%. Manufacturing, usually light industry, now accounts for a higher proportion of employment in rural districts than in many urban areas. But the most significant growth of employment has been in the service sector.

In 1995, over 4.5 million people went to watch racing

The new rural economy of the 1990s is intricately linked with regional, national, even international markets. The key opportunities reside in tourism and recreation, light industry and information technology. Firms relocating in rural areas, or individuals setting up new businesses, are likely to be far more

89

dependent on modern communications, whether of road, cable or the air waves, than in servicing agriculture. In terms of GDP, the fastest growing English regions in the 1980s were East Anglia, the South West and the East Midlands. It is growth based on the small firm. The Rural Development Commission has published figures which show that firms of between 20 and 100 employees, which are considered *small* even though they dwarf many traditional rural concerns, increased in number by nearly 20% in the 1980s in a selection of remoter rural counties compared to just 6% in highly urbanised counties. Such figures mask a number of more complicated issues about the precise location of such businesses, many of which are situated in the sizeable towns located even in predominantly rural counties. Suffice it to say that the much vaunted new rural economy may not always be quite as 'rural' as it is portrayed by some commentators, but that is a topic for another time.

In the past, the rural economy was based firmly on its local natural resource base. People lived and worked in the countryside because of its agriculture or forestry; occasionally because of other natural resources from quarrying and mining. True, the landed classes derived pleasure from country living. But they were a minority of the population and in any case riding to hounds or shooting were natural adjuncts to a rural economy with agriculture at the centre. In the 1990s things are very different.

The transformation of the rural economy has occurred not because of the countryside's natural productive resources, but because people aspire to live there. At the heart of the economic transformation is the phenomenon geographers have dubbed 'counterurbanization'. The 1991 census showed that every single London borough lost population in the decade from 1981, whilst virtually every rural district gained. Counties with a long history of rural depopulation up until the 1960s or 1970s show a sustained and, in many instances, a rapid increase. This does not mean that all rural parishes are increasing in population. Planning restrictions mean that some have remained static or even lost population, but even in those there are likely to have been some newcomers. Indeed, in such villages the pressures of change can seem even greater than elsewhere, with each cottage or small farm coming onto the market eagerly sought by wealthier newcomers prepared to pay a premium for a home in a no-growth village. Farmers, or the estate agents who sell their land, are beguiled by the tempting prospect of selling farm cottages to the highest bidder. Within villages, often characterised in the past by a high percentage of rented accommodation, traditional landlords have been selling for some decades. It is not unheard of, especially in the shire counties of the south, for the farm workers, the odd-job man, the 'domestics' of the affluent new arrivals to live in country towns rather than the villages they work in – a process speeded up by the sale of council houses. Few would regard this as a sensible development and yet measures to ensure that local people can afford to live in the countryside have been piecemeal. In some cases, planning authorities are sympathetic to the need for homes and jobs to be

located in villages. But it is often where the problems are at their worst that the planners seem powerless to help. Villages where the house prices are highest by virtue of their architectural merit, in the Cotswolds for instance, are often the ones where the 'not in my back yard' (NIMBY) syndrome is strongest. The small villages, where job opportunities for local people are most restricted, are usually where new developments are most frowned upon.

By contrast, the most significant population and employment growth is located in the larger villages and country towns. In some cases, growth in these centres has been too fast to allow local communities to properly adapt. Examples of districts with more than 10% population growth in the decade are to be found in Devon, Cornwall, Dorset, Suffolk, Norfolk, Lincolnshire and Cambridgeshire. The countryside is sought out firstly as a desirable place to live and secondly as a good place to locate new, 'clean' businesses. In both instances, amenity concerns are to the fore. All too rarely is the countryside fully recognised as a place of work where its traditional pursuits also need room to develop and adapt to changing circumstances.

What does all this mean to the traditional rural economy based on farming and its support industries? As in most transformations of this sort, there are positive and negative consequences. On the plus side, new people and new firms may mean new markets. Some farmers have bolstered faltering incomes, and even made modest contributions to local employment prospects, by responding to the demand for locally produced food – farm cheeses, pick-your-own, and so forth. Others

"Even in the remotest rural districts of England, agriculture accounts for little more than 6% of employment, and in many of the districts of shire counties it is as little as 3%"

have cashed in by providing shooting, horse riding, war games, farm parks, or locations for businesses in converted farm buildings. The reinvigorated local economy has meant that there are likely to be greater, albeit fluctuating and not always well paid, local job opportunities for members of the farm family. The flight of farmers' sons and daughters from the remoter rural areas to the bright lights for jobs and homes is not as ubiquitous as it once was.

But there is a downside too. Farm business, indeed all traditional rural businesses, are based on property, particularly land, and to expand (or even to survive) may well require investment in fresh property. But setting up the second son on a new farm is increasingly difficult in the light of competition from residential buyers from outside the area. The traditional farming ladder has been rendered all but obsolete, forcing farmers to adopt new strategies, such as unconventional tenures or share farming arrangements with new landholders, to farm land, often to the long-term detriment of both the environment and the well-being or security of the farm family.

Nor can all farmers benefit from opportunities for diversification. Some have neither the capital nor a suitable location. For them, the new rural economy may mean more by way of checks on their business than opportunity. Farmers and farming are much more directly exposed to the scrutiny of non-farmers. The occupants of high-tech businesses and high-tech homes in the countryside do not always look kindly on slurry

spreading in the next field, to modern farm machinery working late at night or early in the morning, to the sound of bird-scarers, to the size and scale of modern farm buildings. Farmers may find themselves strangers in their own land, maligned and misunderstood. Even in the 1960s and early 1970s, as a youngster living in a village in Hampshire – a county where these changes took place early – the majority of farmers located within the parish boundaries were little known to me, a 'newcomer' albeit with a farming background. The farmers didn't attend church or village events. Socially, they seemed entirely peripheral to the village. Only later, when as a student I sought holiday work on various farms, did I hear from  them how they felt the village had little connection with farming and how their work-dominated lives had so little in common with those of the affluent newcomers.

Feeling thus socially marginalised, it is not always easy for farmers to grasp any economic opportunities that might exist within the new rural economy, other than by selling up to the highest bidder. Much the same applies to the agricultural support industries which have often fared worse than farming itself. Amalgamations and closures of feed companies, abattoirs, livestock markets, and farm-dependent businesses have been commonplace in recent decades, in part a response to changes in agriculture itself, but also a consequence of wider economic change, including the high value placed upon the sites which these businesses often occupy.

One of the consequences of the growth and diversification of the rural economy is that, in statistical terms, many traditional economic activities are hidden from view, submerged in broad generic categories. At least agriculture remains a separately identifiable activity and we have a good idea of what is happening to the industry. The story of other sectors is less easy to tell. Field sports are a good example. Various estimates have been made regarding their economic impact but, with inadequate raw data, such estimates are open to dispute. Even when a thorough survey is carried out, the statistics can be used to support the case of both sides of the debate on this contentious matter.

In the early 1990s, I was responsible for directing an economic survey of stag hunting on Exmoor and the Quantocks. Our results were eagerly adopted by proponents and opponents of hunting alike. For the opponents, the fact that just 1.1% of the economically active population of the study area directly or indirectly owed their livelihoods to hunting was heralded as evidence of hunting's economic insignificance. But the proponents could point out, that of the total of 147 jobs, many were concentrated in a very small number of communities on Exmoor, so that locally hunting is of considerable significance.

The new rural economy is so large and diverse that hunting, and shooting too, will inevitably seem small indeed. But if we look at the rural economy in a different way then the story is rather different. In economic terms, field sports might be a relatively small-scale activity alongside so many other growing economic activities, but it is special in so much as it is a non-agricultural activity directly dependent upon the land. Unlike so many rural

businesses which might just as well be based in Bradford, Birmingham or Brighton, field sports have an importance as activities specifically linked to their rural location. Equally importantly, employment in these sectors tends to be the preserve of indigenous rural inhabitants. They comprise a country economy within, or even alongside, the new rural economy.

But field sports as economic activities are scarcely visible to policy makers or to the new rural population, who see only a deeply contentious ethical and political issue. The widespread opposition to field sports is no longer confined to those resident in distant towns, as most hunts and managers of shoots know only too well. Consequently, there is increasing circumspection on the part of hunts or shoots about publicising their activities even within rural England. Whilst this may represent a prudent strategy in the face of opposition, it also renders field sports ever more hidden, both socially and economically.

What is so often forgotten in discussion about the rural economy is that the countryside is home to people with a range of traditional land-based skills. The farm workers, farmers, agricultural contractors, foresters, gamekeepers and hunt employees may be relatively few in number but their impact on the management of rural land and its wildlife, and upon the countryside as enjoyed by so many, is hugely significant. Their activities are lowly paid, especially in comparison with many who have moved to the countryside in recent years. The results of their work are often highly visible and yet socially and economically the land workers are hidden from view. Not every aspect of rural land

"Some farmers have bolstered faltering incomes… by responding to the demand for locally produced food"

management in recent decades is to be applauded. Land workers have no monopoly of virtue and the environmental degradation of many parts of rural England is lamentable. Many country people feel this keenly, lamenting the excesses of modern agriculture. Most, though not all, of what has gone wrong in the countryside can be laid at the door of government and European policies, particularly the economic over-heating of agriculture promoted by the Common Agricultural Policy (CAP).

It is now widely accepted that the CAP must be radically reformed. What is less readily conceded, is that without the flow of CAP money into the countryside, traditional land-based activities and employment will come under even greater pressure. It is foolish merely to assert that fresh opportunities will be afforded by the new rural economy. These opportunities may or may not help the indigenous working population of the countryside. In some instances helpful additional employment will be provided, but in others there will be direct competition between the old and new sectors: competition for housing, business locations and staff. There is already ample anecdotal evidence of the 'old' losing out, with consequent

local shortages of land-based skills – villages where new affluent householders can find no one to lay a hedge or do the gardening; farmers forced to resort to expensive contractors from many miles away to undertake minor repairs on traditional buildings or routine woodland management.

Nor can the market supply every need. So long as there was a large resident workforce in the countryside, attractive natural and man-made features were looked after in the slack periods of the farming year. As soon as farm labour is shed and the farm cottages sold, then there is little economic case for continuing such work. As a result, special schemes have to be devised to encourage farmers to do what they used to do as a normal part of their business: the Hedgerow Incentive Scheme, the Environmentally Sensitive Areas scheme, and so forth. The bill falls to the taxpayer. This is just one of a set of hidden costs, not borne by the market, of the new rural economy. Others include the costs of new roads, traffic pollution, and the pressure on rural services. If the direct beneficiaries of counterurbanization and the new rural economy, perhaps through a more progressive tax

system, were to bear the burden of some of these hidden costs of 'success' then the balance between the old and new rural economies might be somewhat more equitable. The capital thus raised could be ploughed back into rural economies through a partnership between government, preferably local government, and the local and traditional sources of land and capital. What is needed are appropriate rural economic activities which serve the needs of traditional country dwellers and allow for sustainable and environmentally benign development in rural areas.

Michael Winter, a life-long country dweller, is Professor of Rural Economy and Society at the Cheltenham and Gloucester College of Higher Education. Between 1987 and 1993, he directed the Centre for Rural Studies at the Royal Agricultural College, Cirencester. He has researched and written widely on many aspects of rural life, including major studies of socio-economic aspects of farming, hunting and shooting. He is currently directing a study of the impact on the environment of the Common Agricultural Policy.

The Farmer's Case
Robin Page

We live in a strange world. Although Britain has become largely urban and suburban in outlook and inclination, and the prizes given for achievement are presented to city bankers, footballers, lawyers, pop singers and the inventors of new video games, the most important industry in the United Kingdom today continues to be agriculture and the most honourable professions are those of farmer and farm worker. We all need food; we all depend on food, from the most humble carpenter and plumber, to the most self-important yuppie and ego-inflated Member of Parliament.

But since the end of the Second World War farming has changed; it has developed into an industry and many farmers themselves have become industrialists. Growing food has somehow become separated from nature and the farmers themselves have grown remote from their rural communities where once they fulfilled a vital role. It is to Parliament we must look for the reasons why farming has changed.

"Animals… were seen as more than simply 'units of production' or money in the bank"

For generations farming was almost an extension of nature. Men understood the seasons, the soil and the things that shared the land with them; there was a harmony and a sympathy about farming which gave people an understanding and respect for the countryside. Of course there were droughts, rains, good seasons and bad, but these were understood as part of a natural way. Farming was 'agriculture', part skill, part science and part intuition. Animals were important in this too and they were, in the main, treated with respect and seen as more than simply 'units of production' or money in the bank.

Some aspects of modern farming have taken 'respect' away from the land. Landscape is now often seen as an irrelevance, wildlife as an inconvenience and the soil is sometimes regarded merely as a substance that holds the crops up straight while chemicals are poured over them. In other words the 'culture' has been taken out of 'agriculture' and it has become 'agribusiness', an industrial process in which production has become more important than husbandry, and profit margins a more vital component than responsibility. As a result there are large areas of countryside today that are as hostile to wildlife as the Sahara Desert and so unattractive that if John Constable were to return, he would not even bother to take out his paintbrushes.

In his book on his Highgrove estate, HRH the Prince of Wales sums up what has happened perfectly: "As Wendell Berry explains better than I can: "the word 'agriculture', after all, does not mean 'agriscience', much less 'agribusiness'. It means 'cultivation of land'. And cultivation is at the root of the sense both of culture and cult. The ideas of tillage and worship are thus joined in culture. And these words all come from an Indo-European root meaning both 'to revolve' and 'to dwell'. To live, to survive on the earth, to care for the soil, and to worship, are all bound up." But we have broken the cycle and by our arrogant denial of the almost mystical relationship between tillage and worship (as if we were too sophisticated and clever for such a primitive and irrelevant concept) we have nearly destroyed the cultural element of farming in Britain."

"by our arrogant denial of the almost mystical relationship between tillage and worship… we have nearly destroyed the cultural element of farming in Britain"

It has been our Members of Parliament who have destroyed this cultural element of farming; they have placed 'production' before husbandry, morality and responsibility. For centuries Parliament had a large majority of members from country backgrounds. It is true that many of them were only there because of privilege and wealth, but there was a basic understanding of agriculture. With the advent of the Industrial Revolution, the make-up of Parliament began to change; from 1945 change turned into total transformation. Although about 80% of our land today is made up of farmed countryside, only about 11% of our MPs have the slightest interest in farming and the issues of the countryside.

As a rule, allowing for heart attacks, and runaway buses, we have about 651 MPs. Approximately 12 of them are farmers, or have farming interests (most of these are directors of farming companies of the type that rarely get mud on their boots and whose Range Rovers are without tow-bars). Then there are about another 60 who claim that one of their 'special interests' is 'rural affairs', yet when most of them speak on practical and important countryside issues their depth of knowledge is poor. A recent incident clearly shows Parliament's ignorance and indifference on country matters. When the Secretary of State for the Environment, John Gummer, introduced his

long-awaited Rural White Paper to the House of Commons in 1995, he did so to a largely deserted House. He was surrounded by row upon row of green, empty seats. Parliament was not interested.

The problems with farming began immediately after the Second World War. Our politicians quite rightly said that Britain must never be hungry again; we must increase production and we must try to become self-sufficient. To achieve these aims agriculture must be supported with grants and subsidies. This is when the dredge, drain, rip-out and cut-down mentality came into farming; the politicians assumed that the increase in production would come primarily from an increase in the amount of land under production. Consequently, grants and subsidies were given to enable hedges to be ripped out, spinneys to be bulldozed down and water meadows to be drained and ploughed. The effect on our landscape was, and is, startling and the effect on farmers was just as great. A 'culture' of 'farming for subsidies' developed, in which the year's cropping plan did not follow a rotation or a system of sustainable husbandry; it followed the course of maximum financial return, aided and abetted by subsidies for 'improvement' and increased production.

What they failed to realise was that agricultural production was set to increase anyway. With technological advance and giant steps forward in the chemistry, biology and botany of farming, yields were set to improve. In 1971, when the brook running through our small family farm was 'cleaned out', enabling water meadows that had been water meadows for

hundreds of years to be brought into arable production, I complained bitterly. I asked for a reason when it was already clear that Europe was heading towards over-production. Those who complained were accused of being out-of-touch reactionaries, or people who simply did not understand the needs of modern agriculture. Almost as soon as the drag-lines had disappeared, hedges were being ripped out and the water meadows were being incorporated into larger arable fields, signalling the disappearance of free-range livestock, as well as an area rich in wildlife. It was all government-induced and paid for; now much of that same land has been taken out of production again under set-aside and 'Stewardship', in return for more subsidies. So, the taxpayer pays to put land into production; he then pays to take it out of production – it is known as long-term agricultural planning.

With agricultural advance, production would have gone up anyway and with a system of environmental protection and subsidies – financial rewards for retaining hedgerows and water meadows, etc – we could have had the best of both worlds: increased production and an attractive landscape rich in wildlife. Indeed, if present agricultural subsidies were linked to environmental action the whole of the British landscape could be transformed and invigorated, almost overnight. The message of the last few years is one of lost opportunities, caused not simply by the lack of vision of our Members of Parliament, and those who advise them, but by a basic lack of knowledge and understanding.

As a result of the reckless policies of 'rewards for wrecking', the traditional countryside was transformed in just a few years. Between 1946 and 1970

Norfolk lost half its hedgerows – 8000 miles – while Huntingdonshire lost 90% – 5000 miles – during the same period. The story was the same countrywide with 150 000 miles of hedges being bulldozed into oblivion. 95% of Britain's traditional lowland hay meadows went, as well as 80% of chalk and limestone grassland. At the same time 37 000 acres a year have been lost to development and afforestation. Field size has increased, rivers and streams have been turned into drainage channels; many farms have become factories.

Another more recent nonsense sums up ignorance of farming just as well. There is, quite rightly, much concern at the moment about the transportation of live animals. What many people do not realise is that a large number of farmers share their anxieties. But the situation is not the fault of the farming community; over the last few years hundreds of slaughterhouses have been closed down throughout Britain under absurd EU legislation. Christopher Booker wrote articles condemning the scandal, and in my small way, with the pen and in direct debate with the then Secretary of State for Agriculture, John Gummer, I tried to alert the public and reverse the process. We failed. Now, not only are animals exported live across the Channel, but many animals travel even further within Britain simply to be killed – a fact that the protesters seem incapable of understanding. Two years ago my sheep, produced traditionally and almost organically, were picked up in a huge transporter, with three levels, for slaughter. After leaving the farm the lorry was going on to other farms in Cambridgeshire and Bedfordshire picking up cattle and pigs as it went, before finally returning to an abattoir in North Norfolk. In other words, my animals would be on the lorry all day. I was so concerned that I seriously considered giving up keeping sheep. Fortunately, I have found a small abattoir (the last one) that will take my animals. It means they are in the trailer for only 15 minutes. It is the same trailer that takes them from pasture to pasture and brings the ram each autumn and so there is no stress whatsoever. Consequently this year my conscience has been perfectly clear, and the lamb and mint sauce tasted good.

If I am painting a dismal picture of farming it is because the industrialisation of food production is a depressing story. It is a story in which farming has become entirely a matter of production, and agricultural policies are driven almost entirely by production encouragement or production control.

Fortunately, however, there are many farmers who have not been taken in by fashion and who are not interested in farming simply as a means of getting their third BMW. They are still interested in farming as 'agriculture' and they are proud of the 'culture'. This pride in tradition, landscape, wildlife and, yes, 'profit' can best be seen in the family farm, where the farm has passed through the generations and where there is a real feeling of pride and continuity. The grandfather wants the farm to go to his son and on to his grandson in as good a condition as when he first inherited it. It is strange how these feelings of responsibility and continuity are best seen on small farms and large estates. A County Council Trees Officer once told me that the farms most interested in tree planting were the small family farms and the large estates, both keen to develop and maintain landscapes. The problems were

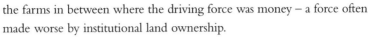

*"We want farming
policies that link care for
the environment with
production of food"*

the farms in between where the driving force was money – a force often made worse by institutional land ownership.

This was confirmed to me two years ago when I was invited to Wadebridge in Cornwall to talk at the 25th Anniversary Celebrations of the Cornish Farming and Wildlife Advisory Group. The meeting was packed with working farmers, most driving muddied pick-up trucks. At a similar celebratory meeting held in Cambridgeshire – the centre for unacceptable modern farming – there were only a handful of farmers present. The farmers of Cornwall live their conservation; some of the farmers of East Anglia's prairie lands treat it as an optional extra.

But there is another segment of the farming community that still retains attractive hedgerows and landscapes. On their land, otters, orchids and barn owls can sometimes be found among traditional landscapes, while farming is nevertheless carried out on a commercial scale. These are the landowners who hunt, shoot and fish. Indeed it is possible to drive around the countryside pointing out the farms where profit is the only driving force, and those where country sports are an important aspect of their land management. One will be a prairie on a lost, manicured landscape; the other will be a productive farm with hedges, spinneys and wetland. The simple message is that farmland kept suitable for the fox, pheasant and partridge is also suitable for wildflowers, songbirds, butterflies and a host of other wildlife. Consequently it is the hunting, shooting, fishing farmer that is doing much for wildlife in the general countryside.

From this it goes almost without saying that there is currently a hard core of MPs, from all parties, dedicated to the abolition of 'cruel blood sports'. It is another indication of how our suburban and urban rulers have

become separated from the land and from reality. The conservation pluses of 'blood sports' are grass margins, conservation headlands, coverts, shelter belts, woods, spinneys, grassland, wetland, flight ponds, beetle banks, etc, etc. It represents the largest conservation input on the general countryside today. Three years ago I set up The Countryside Restoration Trust. Our aim is to buy land that had been over-intensively farmed and to restore it. We want to show that commercial farming, wildlife and landscape can co-exist. Our task is being made easier by the work that had been carried out earlier by the Game Conservancy for 'sport'. It has shown clearly and scientifically that habitat which benefits game is also of benefit to the skylark, the lapwing, butterflies and wildflowers.

What we need now is politicians to for once forget their rhetoric and image and concentrate on what needs to be done. We want farming policies that link care for the environment with the production of food. We want a financial structure that will keep the small family farmers farming and, most important of all, we want the vision that will put the 'culture' back into agriculture.

Robin Page, the well known author, television personality and conservationist, lives and farms in Cambridgeshire. He contributes a fortnightly column to The Daily Telegraph *and is currently presenting* One Man and His Dog *on television.*

Details of The Countryside Restoration Trust can be found on page 185.

"The grandfather wants the farm to go to his son and on to his grandson in as good a condition as when he first inherited it"

A Politically Incorrect View
Willy Poole

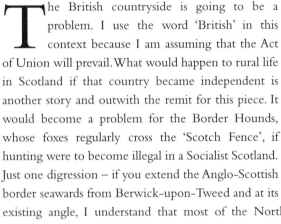

"The BSE scare has been bred by political bungling out of journalistic hysteria"

The British countryside is going to be a problem. I use the word 'British' in this context because I am assuming that the Act of Union will prevail. What would happen to rural life in Scotland if that country became independent is another story and outwith the remit for this piece. It would become a problem for the Border Hounds, whose foxes regularly cross the 'Scotch Fence', if hunting were to become illegal in a Socialist Scotland. Just one digression – if you extend the Anglo-Scottish border seawards from Berwick-upon-Tweed and at its existing angle, I understand that most of the North Sea oil would remain English.

The British countryside and its way of life is under threat – no one can be of any doubt about that and it is partly the fault of us aboriginal countrymen. Look at our reaction to the BSE debacle. The BSE scare has been bred by political bungling out of journalistic hysteria. There is also little doubt that many honest, hard-working, country people are going to be ruined and unemployed because of political ineptitude. What have we country people done about it? Nothing! I simply cannot imagine this situation in France, for instance – herds of cows would have been loosed onto motorways, there would be blood in Downing Street and no MP would dare set foot in the countryside. But then no other

European government would have allowed a situation like this to develop. The British government knows that it can continue to ignore the wishes and well-being of country people because the rural vote is tiny and because the English countryman has been supine for too long. We have become an ignored and despised minority and we all know what happens to them.

In the past I have often compared the plight of the aboriginal English countryman to that of the Native America 'Indians'. The fact that we were there first will avail us nothing in the coming struggle for survival. We are numerically and politically weak and we have refused to stand up for ourselves.

Numerical weakness we can do little about. In the eighteenth and nineteenth centuries, the lords of the land drove out the peasantry in the country by means of the Enclosures Acts. These acts destroyed the common land and the livelihoods, however precarious, of those who relied on their 'Common Rights' for grazing and other small necessities: "The law will punish man or woman, who steals a goose from off the common, but lets the greater felon loose, who steals the common from the goose". The disgruntled peasantry were driven into the newly spreading towns as fodder for the Industrial Revolution, where they became

even more disgruntled and eventually founded the Labour Party. The same thing did not happen in other European countries where the political power of the peasantry remains strong. This is especially so under the Napoleonic Code in Inheritance where each child in a family inherits equally. So you have a farm that is worked by Alphonse and Yvette (or, as it might be, Helmut and Mitzi) but it is *owned* by many degrees of brothers, sisters, aunts, uncles and cousins. "All Rabbit's friends and relations" may live and work in towns, but they *vote* for the family farm. In England we have 150 years worth of generations who have had no contact with, or interest in, the countryside. For many years 'Urban Person' was quite content to avoid the countryside, which he regarded as nasty, brutish and backward. It was also extremely difficult to get to. This has changed.

Until recent times, the aboriginal were protected by powerful political champions. Not only was the House of Lords full of landed

interests, but so also was the Commons with the 'Knights of the Shires'. Mrs Thatcher did for them. The modern Conservative Party, to whom countrymen still vainly look for support, is more urban now than it ever has been. The National Farmers' Union has been totally emasculated politically. One of its officials told me that they had written off Westminster anyway and now concentrate their efforts on Brussels.

So where are we at? We have an overcrowded country which is something like 95% urban in thought, word and deed. To these people, the countryside is a backward, muddy and bloody place, occupied by a people so different to them in every way that they can be regarded as difficult and backward foreigners with some very nasty habits. Something must be done.

Urban man is no longer content with his cities and, when you see what he has done to them, this is hardly surprising. Now Urban man is a car owner he wants to escape from his battery cage. The place he most wants to go is the countryside, but he does not like the countryside as it is — it does not conform to what he thinks it should be like. What Urban man wants is a gigantic theme park in which he can walk where he wants, ride his motorcycle, park his car, throw away his beer cans and generally do what he damned well likes. He wants the picturesque villages which he can sanitise into nice dormitories with street lighting, but without nasty untidy locals. The locals can be confined to the council estates, if there are any, or they can go and live in nice high-rise

The conservation pluses of "blood sports" are many

slums in the city, or they can go to perdition and oblivion – who cares! It is possible that a few well behaved ones might be allowed to remain – to bake cakes, pose in smock frocks and knuckle their foreheads to the new gentry of the urban middle classes. A few token farms may be kept for visitors to visit, but the concept of the countryside as a living, breathing workplace will be consigned to the dustbin of history along with the aboriginal inhabitants. The idea of farming as a major food-producing industry will be regarded as nonsense – food comes from supermarkets and all farmers are subsidised rogues.

You can see this attitude hard at work in the 'National Parks' in England and Wales. The very title is a snare and a delusion. The term 'National Park' encourages people to think of something like Wimbledon Common writ large. Many townspeople think that the land is in public ownership and that they have every right to do as they wish there. When it is pointed out that most of the land is privately owned and worked, the Urbans become somewhat miffed and go and pull down another stone wall. The National Park Committees (NPCs) encourage the Urbans in this casuistry, which is very much one that they would like to make reality. NPCs with their make-up of County Council, District Council and Department of Environment appointees (recommended by the Countryside Commission) have a record of totally ignoring the needs of the locals in favour of the

tourists. You have only to look at the list of bodies whom the NPCs consult: you will find everything from Gay Liberation to the Ramblers' Association, but you will not find the NFU or the CLA. After some considerable political pressure from the grass roots, Parish Councils are going to be represented on NPCs and this will be a step forward. Many areas are forming ARCs – Associations of Rural Communities – whose aim is to foster the economic and social well-being of the locals in those areas. These associations are a step forward and, like the 'Campaign for Hunting' and the 'Countryside Movement', a belated attempt to redress the balance and to make sure that the voice of the indigenous countryman is still heard. It is to be hoped that all of this is not too little and too late.

Country people have voices and if they do not want to lose their way of life then they must use them.

Willy Poole lives and farms in Northumberland. He was a Master of Foxhounds for 25 years but is now reduced to journalism. He is a regular contributor to many country publications, including writing a fortnightly column for The Daily Telegraph.

Changing Pressures
Richard Ehrman

To those who live in cities, the countryside lobby can seem extraordinarily unconvincing. The country, after all, is a pleasant place to live and, nowadays, a prosperous one as well. In stark contrast to many other parts of Europe, where migration to the cities is still the rule, the rural population in this country is growing. In this country unemployment is generally lower in rural areas, and the price of housing often higher, than in nearby towns.

So why, those condemned to urban grime might ask, did the government feel moved to publish in 1995 a long, expensive White Paper supposedly addressing the problems of the countryside? We have never had a paper on the problems of the suburbs, despite all the horrors of 'downsizing' and negative equity.

The Rural White Paper never quite had the nerve to say as much, but in the countryside now it is success that is widely thought to have become the problem. The lobbies that count are not those, like the Rural Development Commission, who want to promote rural growth, but rather the likes of the CPRE who want to stop it in its tracks.

In a crowded country, only the most extreme free marketeer would argue that development in rural areas should not be controlled. Even those ogres, the developers, accept the need for a proper planning system. There, however, the consensus breaks down and the scare stories take over: that 21 new towns the size of Milton Keynes will be needed over the next 20 years, or – to quote another recent example – that the urban

area of England will double over the next century. Of course economic growth entails development and population shift. But even during the 1950s and 60s, when redevelopment and new towns were all the rage, we never saw anything on this scale.

For the discussion to be conducted like this is not just unrealistic, it is also sloppy to the point of unscrupulousness. The conservationists never seem to question the factual basis on which they demand that the liberty of others to live or drive where they want should be restricted. There is this enormous fear that the slightest relaxation of 'not in my back yard' (NIMBY) vigilance would lead to a massive invasion of the countryside. That was widely assumed to be the case in the 1980s, but is it still really so – if, indeed, it ever was?

Conservationists need to take a long, hard look at the realities of the 1990s. Now that house prices have fallen, so has the appetite for buying and selling them. The composition of households, too, is changing. Because we marry later, divorce more frequently and then live longer than we did, more people now live on their own.

More new homes will be needed. But older people who want to be near the shops, and single people who need to be close to work, are less likely to want to move out of town than traditional families with children. A lot of the new homes will be flats in towns, many converted from existing buildings. This is already happening. For the first time in half a century the population of inner London is beginning to increase.

Just as the conservationists often overrate the traditional threats to rural tranquillity, so they tend to underrate the new ones. Road building, for instance, is now diminishing rapidly, but the public desire for a day out grows apace. Even those who have no desire to live in the country still want to visit it and to do things – fish, sail, play golf or whatever – when they get there. In theory these might all be considered 'green' activities, but they have an enormous impact on the countryside. In five years at the end of the 1980s an area the size of Greater Manchester is reckoned to have been turned over to nearly 400 golf courses.

With these visitors come strong, urban opinions on how the countryside should be run. Take, for example, that quintessentially townie organisation, the Ramblers' Association which, backed to some extent by Labour, now demands a right to access to all land – private and public – and makes no secret of its distrust of landowners. "We are fed up," its chairman once said, "of being kept out of our own backyard." Farming too has become an object of urban attack, as field sports have been for sometime. A generation that buys its meat plastic-wrapped in supermarkets and knows animals largely through the characters of Walt Disney is ready fodder for the 'animal rights' and anti-field sports propaganda spewed out by urban-based activists.

How should the people who live and work in the country react to all of this? For those who live in towns to expect the countryside to be run as a great public park for their recreation is clearly unrealistic. But to demand, as the rural lobbies are wont to, that the countryside should be both left in peace and subsidised is hardly realistic either.

This is something farmers in particular need to take on board. Their business has been built around subsidy from the Common Agricultural Policy. The beef crisis not withstanding, the CAP has done British farmers very nicely indeed. But it is far too expensive, and reform will catch up with it one day. When it does, farmers may well face a choice of either losing subsidy or adopting more environmentally sensitive methods. To most people, whose weekly shopping bills are massively inflated by the current arrangements, that will sound a reasonable trade-off. Farmers should be thinking hard about how they can adapt to CAP reform. Realism demands flexibility.

The same goes for development. Conservationists always argue that if the inner cities were made attractive and public transport improved, the pressure for development in the countryside could be directed elsewhere. But not only would that require public spending on a scale to bankrupt Croesus, it also assumes that a society which runs on wheels can somehow be weaned off its love affair with the car. Neither seems likely.

What the rural lobbies could demand, more convincingly, is that quality should take precedence over quantity. Amazingly, whilst vast energy is devoted to debating how much development should be allowed and where, the quality of the end product hardly enters into the equation.

The results are all too plain to see – and hear. Over-crammed, badly designed housing estates, built of cheap materials, disfigure our towns and villages. Much of the opposition to new building is due to its sheer ugliness. Noisy road surfaces and poor or non-existent screening exacerbate the impact of motorways.

We could have less intrusive roads. They would cost more, but given the need to protect the countryside without throttling the economy it would be money well spent. We could have more sympathetic development too. Instead of frightening people with talk of massive new towns, the planners should learn to think small. They should drop their long-standing opposition to new villages of traditional type and scale. Prince Charles' plans at Poundbury may have got off to a slow start, but they

show the sort of thing that can be done. There are plenty of redundant military bases which would provide suitable sites.

Better quality building need not necessarily cost buyers a lot more. Even now, after years of recession in the property market, an acre whose use is changed from agriculture to housing can (thanks to the workings of the planning system) increase a hundredfold in price overnight. Much more of that money should be spent on improved design and materials. If builders and landowners were told that quality was the key to planning permission, they would have a real incentive to build it into their schemes.

Over the last five years the problems facing the countryside have changed – to a far greater degree than many of the rural lobby groups seem to realise. There will always be pressure for road building and housing, but it is less than it was. Other pressures are, however, increasing, particularly on farming and traditional country sports. To counter these, the rural lobbies need to devote more attention to educating people in

towns about how the country actually works. They should put more effort into promoting environmentally sensitive designs for roads and buildings. Farmers need to respond to public concern about intensive agriculture, and argue their case more forcefully against the 'animal rights' zealots.

The prospect of a Labour government, anti-hunting and much less favourably inclined to rural interests in general than the Conservatives, makes the need for the countryside lobbies to update their thinking even more urgent. Some, like the new Countryside Movement, do seem to realise that a new direction is needed. The Access 2000 initiative, launched by the Countryside Landowners' Association to promote voluntary access to land and alert the Labour Party and the public to the problems of a 'right to roam', is another example of what might be done.

The social, political and economic forces that impinge on traditional rural life cannot just be frozen. Nor can they be ignored. But with a modicum of realism and flexibility they could be mitigated.

Richard Ehrman lives in Oxfordshire and writes leading articles for The Daily Telegraph. *He was until recently the paper's Chief Leader Writer. In the 1980s he served as Special Adviser to the Department of Employment, and later to the Northern Ireland Office.*

"For those who live in towns to expect the countryside to be run as a great public park for their recreation is clearly unrealistic"

The Common Agricultural Policy

Nick Way

O ver the next few years British farmers face changes in their marketplace and in government policies as great as any in the previous century. Nor should we expect the Common Agricultural Policy (CAP) to continue in its present form. In ten years it may be unrecognisable, compared to the monolithic instrument for production support which prompted so much criticism in the 1980s.

It is not that our European partners have suddenly accepted the argument, familiar in Britain, that the CAP is too costly to consumers and taxpayers. The CAP is seen on the continent as one of Europe's successes, responsible for the managed transition from food shortage and peasant poverty in the 1950s to plenty and high productivity now. The pressures that drive change come from all over Europe, not just from Britain. The number of farmers is falling; in France to below one million. The number of owners of land, incidentally, is not. Interest in encouraging farmers to provide a wider range of 'products' to the public – including environmental land management – is spreading, not just in the northern states, but also through France to Spain, Portugal and Italy.

Throughout Europe, the politicians and public are looking to the CAP to meet new objectives, not just to provide high-quality food, but also to meet environmental demands and to help knit together rural communities. There is a growing feeling in the European Commission and in other member states that the CAP will need to be reshaped if it is to do this.

"Over the next few years British farmers face changes in their marketplace and in government policies as great as any in the previous century"

At the same time, the greater exposure of European agriculture to worldwide competition, the prospect of enlargement of the European Union to the east and greater trade links with its Mediterranean neighbours, together with forthcoming re-negotiations of the EU budget and then GATT in the coming years, means that there are plenty of reasons to predict that Europe will want significant, but managed, change in the CAP.

The UK has plenty to offer in the developing debate, and there is great interest in the initiatives we ourselves have introduced. Our environmentally sensitive areas, and now our countryside stewardship schemes are being used as models in other member states. The possibility exists for Britain to have a major positive influence in any reshaping of the CAP.

Amidst this sanguine approach, some cautionary points must be made. First, these 'agri-environmental' measures are not what currently lubricates the rural economy. The CAP pumps about £3 billion annually into our countryside and the communities who live and work there. Unlike water, the money flows both upstream and downstream. Agriculture may now employ less than 5% of the whole of Europe's working population, but its position at the centre of rural land use, and rural life, must not be underestimated. The effect of the beef crisis on the economy of livestock-producing areas underlined this. In the UK, expenditure on all the agri-environmental measures will amount to £100 million per year by the end of the 1990s. Compared to

CAP production-related support, this is small beer. The effects of removal of that support on the economy and social structures in rural areas, and on the stewardship of the countryside, would be devastating. Anyone who doubts the underpinning role of farming in our countryside needs only to look at the scale and extent of the BSE scare on livestock-rearing areas, with up to 100 000 jobs involved in one way or another in the British beef industry, let alone dairying.

So the question remains as to how to develop the CAP into a broader European Rural Policy, whilst at the same time allowing room for local enterprise and encouraging national and local policies which promote the diverse economic activity in rural areas.

At the European level, one way forward would be for the CAP, over a period of years, to develop better targeted policies to meet the specific objectives of competitive agriculture, sustainable environmental land management, and thriving rural communities. If the choice of economic instruments is to be between a market approach and a supply control approach which carries a high level of government and European intervention, the market approach is surely the better way forward for the efficient structure of British farming. That said, there will continue to need to be special help for the hills and other less favoured areas of Europe.

If support related to production is to be reduced, the expansion of the funds available for stewardship-type schemes is going to have to be

considerable. Farmers and landowners simply will not be able to provide environmental management of the countryside if it is not profitable to do so. But, increasingly, this is what the public says it wants and is prepared to pay for, alongside a plentiful supply of wholesome food. There are signs that the public will be happy to pay, as long as it can see that it is getting results. In that climate, producers will be happy to get nearer to their customers both in providing food and in conserving the countryside.

The CAP must also assist in promoting new businesses and investment in non-agricultural activities in the countryside, since it will be these jobs which will employ the majority of the rural population. Funds to the so-called Objective 5b areas (the parts of the EU that are eligible for EU rural development aid) must be transmitted better to individual businesses, but attention must be paid to the prospects for small businesses in all parts of the country, not just in designated areas, since it is these businesses which are the engine for growth, jobs and incomes in the countryside.

Whilst Europe will continue to have the major role in determining the overall level of support in the CAP, and in enforcing an open single market, there are many policy areas in which the British Government can play a positive role. Country people have the same needs for jobs, houses and services as their urban counterparts. These needs will be met only if the

"Funds for the so-called Objective 5b areas… must be transmitted better to individual businesses"

rural economy is allowed to thrive, if appropriate development is encouraged, not stifled, and if the particular characteristics of rural areas are recognised. Rural communities tend to be smaller and more interdependent than urban populations and, of course, they are often more remote. One result is that services, such as education, may be more expensive to provide in many rural areas.

So it is crucial that government ensures an approach to rural development which integrates, for example, jobs, housing and transport, so that communities can survive and be self-reliant. Planning policy should enable, not just control; housing provision must be looked at alongside development decisions, and so must the provision of schools, transport and other services. The Government's White Papers, *Rural England* and *A Working Countryside in Wales* recognise that rural life consists of this mosaic of diverse activities and that the picture comes only from the whole. Key priorities emerge: a profitable agriculture; development of the stewardship schemes; more flexible planning; a review of the need to streamline taxation of small businesses; sufficient provision of mixed housing; an adequate transport network, including roads; more diverse training; getting on top of rural crime; and not least, a mechanism for ensuring that all parts of government whose actions affect the countryside begin to take the needs of their rural constituents properly into account.

Again, there are lessons to be learnt from the 1996 BSE and beef crisis. Not only did that demonstrate the importance of agriculture in the economy of the countryside and, nationally, the desirability of farmers and landowners making closer links with their customers in future, it also demonstrated within government that many departments, for example

DTI and Employment, not just Agriculture, have an interest in the economic health of the countryside.

John Donne reminded us that no man is an island. It is because so many different communities, businesses and activities in the countryside depend on each other that the CAP and government policies must accommodate all aspects of rural life. More than that, those who live in our towns and cities are as reliant on a thriving and attractive countryside as countryfolk are on those towns and cities for their markets and their cultural diversions.

Nick Way is Political Adviser at the Country Landowners' Association (CLA). After graduating from Clare College, Cambridge in Economics, he worked in the Ministry of Agriculture, Fisheries and Food from 1978 to 1989. Amongst other things he was Private Secretary to Peggy Fenner MP, Junior Minister with responsibilities for food, exports, animal health and welfare from 1982 to 1984. He also worked on CAP and agricultural trade issues. Since 1989, he has been Political Adviser at the CLA, organising the CLA's political lobbying in Westminster, Brussels and Strasbourg, and developing the CLA's contacts with the main political parties.

The Need To Educate

Dawn Goodfellow

'The Environment' is a very topical issue. There are a number of well-funded national and international organisations producing sophisticated, high–quality resources for teachers to use in the classroom, most from a very 'protectionist' point of view. Many schemes and campaigns have been set up in recent years to encourage schools to develop their grounds, and encourage recycling and re-use of waste; whilst television and press coverage frequently centres on global environmental issues, such as the 'greenhouse effect' and the destruction of tropical rainforests.

Over the last ten years, schools, business and industry have recognised the need for a much closer partnership if young people are to develop, during their school careers, the skills and attitudes necessary for adult and working life. Many individual companies and sectors of industry have begun to invest substantially in specialist personnel, resource materials and programmes designed to make both teachers and students aware of their industry. The purpose of this investment is to enhance teachers' and students' economic awareness and understanding of the place of wealth creation within our society. It is further intended to create an understanding of, and sympathy for, particular companies or sectors of industry amongst tomorrow's workforce and consumers.

However, despite this growing interest in environmental issues and economic and industrial understanding, the contribution of rural Britain to both our environment and economy has been largely

"No longer do school trips consist of a one-off 'nice day out'"

neglected. Research conducted by a number of organisations has shown that environmental education frequently deals solely with global issues and the built environment. Where countryside issues do appear on the school curriculum, they are taught in a very fragmented way. What is lacking is the overview of the British countryside as a living, working environment.

It is a very complex combination of factors that has led to this state of affairs. Many we are all extremely familiar with: decline in employment in traditional land-based industries; a very small percentage of our population living in rural areas; increased mobility contributing to a change in the structure of rural communities. All these factors have contributed to the ever-widening gulf between town and country dweller. Changes in the way we shop and eat have further removed the vast majority of the population from the source of what they are consuming.

Added to these influences are specific educational issues. Most teachers at both primary and secondary level will have come from an urban background. If they haven't, they will almost certainly have been trained by someone who has. They will therefore frequently have no idea of the realities of the countryside, or how to use it as a resource for learning. A lack of knowledge on their own part will, understandably, lead to a lack of confidence or reluctance to tackle the topic.

Teachers surveyed about their views on teaching about the countryside often commented on the lack of balanced, accessible material available to them. Much of the material they receive is produced by lobby groups and is therefore biased in some way. It also lacks relevance to the National Curriculum and is not in a form which teachers could use easily in the classroom. The fact that most of the groups producing materials are 'single-issue' bodies further serves to promote the fragmented approach to the countryside so many teachers are taking.

Teachers are now charged, since the advent of the National Curriculum, with delivering a prescribed content in each subject. Any materials produced must take full account of the National Curriculum requirements to be of any use to teachers in the classroom. Having to meet these very specific targets within subjects has also meant that

teachers have to be much more objective about the way in which they use activities such as school visits to support classroom teaching. No longer do school trips consist of a one-off 'nice day out'; they must have a clear relevance to what is currently being taught to be justifiable. This has led to a marked downturn in attendance by school parties at the major shows and events such as farm open days. These events are obviously a valuable opportunity to educate and interest both teachers and students in countryside issues. It is therefore important to market them to the educational community in a way that clearly demonstrates all the curriculum opportunities they offer and encourages teachers to use the medium of the countryside as a teaching resource.

Many people stereotypically regard teachers as left-wing or 'anti' everything. In fact, they form a reasonable cross-section of our population and have a mandatory responsibility to provide children with balanced information and the necessary skills to make their own reasoned judgements about controversial issues. This is obviously a very complex problem, since many different, often highly 'respectable', groups will put forward opposing versions of the 'facts'. The teacher is then left, possibly with no personal background knowledge, to distinguish fact from opinion.

In the moral and spiritual guidance discussion paper produced by the National Curriculum Council in 1993, the following comment is made: "Society permits, even if it does not promote, a range of behaviour which is considered wrong by some, often many, of its 'members'. Examples would include drinking alcohol, smoking and gambling as well as divorce, abortion and what are called blood sports. Pupils have to make up their own minds on these and other issues, some of which will arise as part of the planned curriculum and some as a result of immediate events. The task of schools, in partnership with the home, is to furnish pupils with the knowledge and the ability to question and reason which will enable them to develop their own value system and to make responsible decisions on such matters."

Many of the traditional support mechanisms or incentives for teaching about rural activities have also been collapsing in the recent past. Following the incorporation of the agricultural colleges, and their departure from the Local Authority structure, their previous links with local schools have in many cases deteriorated. The result has been that much of the school liaison/development work, supporting teachers with visits to college farms or providing careers and course information has decreased in many areas. The courses being offered by the

agricultural colleges reflect the change in attitude towards our countryside: that agriculture and farming are no longer fashionable. A large number of colleges have dropped the word 'agriculture' altogether from their titles. The courses on offer also reflect a change in demand. There has been a trend in recent years away from the traditional agriculture and horticulture courses, towards subjects such as tourism and leisure, environmental studies and countryside management.

Rural science in secondary schools has seen a dramatic decline, with many schools no longer offering it at all. The number of examination syllabi dealing with rural activity at Key Stage 4 (14–16 year olds) has likewise declined. The courses have become less popular with students, and are expensive for schools to run. The number of schools with their own farm units has dropped during the last five to ten years. Cornwall, a county most of us would perceive to be very rural, is an example of this. Until four years ago rural science was taught in 31 of the county's 33 secondary schools, and 95% of those had plants or stock on site. Now only six or seven teach the subject and only three have farm units. The number of Young Farmers' Clubs attached to schools stood at 112 in 1984 and had reduced to 40 in 1994.

In the past, partly because of the large number of countryside factions and interests, there had never appeared to be a cohesive force which sought to present a 'united front' or image of the countryside in its entirety. However, in order to have the greatest impact on the population as a whole, it is essential to gain access to the state-maintained schooling system in the UK. For any initiative to gain credibility and acceptance with the educational community, it must be designed in partnership with education professionals and addressed to teachers and their professional development. It must be relevant to the needs of the teacher and very easily accessible. This is an expensive exercise, requiring time to develop it properly, and at a time when the opponents of many countryside activities are so well resourced, a pooling of funds would mean a far more effective approach.

There is another aspect which makes this united approach so critical. Our countryside as it appears today has been wholly created by man's activities. It is the diversity of those activities that have contributed to one of the most beautiful and varied landscapes in the world. Until a very basic understanding is gained of the integral nature

of all those activities, it is impossible to start educating effectively about any single issue. If the rural environment is perceived as some sort of 'theme park', rather than a series of industries operating under the same economic constraints as any other sector, it becomes impossible to understand the choices facing those responsible for its management.

It is high time that quality educational materials and schemes which promote the countryside in all its aspects are made readily accessible to teachers. It is very clear, that some groups who oppose some countryside activities are very well funded and have adopted a very sophisticated and professional approach to education in order to convey their point of view for some considerable length of time. Until the materials and schemes are available, schools and teachers cannot be blamed for ignoring rural Britain, or for providing what some people perceive to be an inaccurate view. What is also required is pressure on governments to prioritise environmental education and, in particular, the place of rural Britain within it.

There are many ways in which individuals can influence education on a local level. In recent years, much of the day-to-day management has been devolved from Local Education Authorities to schools. In practical terms, this means that most schools now manage their own finances and can make individual decisions over what sort of resources they purchase. It also means that the boards of governors have much more power over

"A substantial number of parents of children in school today have no knowledge or experience of the countryside."

the way that a school is run. Schools should now all have development plans which detail for a set period (usually two years) the content of the curriculum and how it will be delivered. Governors of both rural and urban schools should be questioning whether issues about rural Britain are being addressed and how they are being addressed. Governors should also be examining the sorts of materials that teachers are using, and the source of those materials. If material that expresses a certain point of view is to be used in a classroom then it should be used alongside materials expressing opposing points of view, and used in such a way as to allow children to reach their own conclusions. Parents should also feel able to contribute to this process, commenting or feeding back concerns if they feel that their child has been given unbalanced or inaccurate information.

Education has frequently been viewed as a long-term and expensive strategy, particularly when votes are needed in Parliament in the very short term. However, its short-term benefits should not be under-

estimated. A substantial number of parents of children in school today have no knowledge or experience of the countryside. Equally, approximately only 23% of our adult population reads a quality newspaper on a regular basis. A lot of information that might never reach many adults travels home from school with children, particularly when they are motivated by an exciting topic. In one of the schools that trialled Countryside Foundation materials, the teacher

specifically commented on the level of interest it had generated amongst parents who did not normally involve themselves in their children's education.

Children and young people also form a large and influential consumer group, their tastes and desires frequently affecting family spending. An example of this is the rise in the number of young people turning away from eating meat. There is, therefore, an economic argument for educating them about the realities of our relationship with animals and the responsibilities that come with that relationship. They should be aware, in taking such decisions, of what our countryside would look like without livestock farming, and what could happen to animal welfare if the commercial rewards for keeping livestock were removed. The lives of most young people have become so sanitised, and death such a taboo subject within our society, that the very emotive claims and arguments of the animal rights movement seem very attractive. The movement has been very successful in making its message fashionable with and appealing to young people, by using celebrities with whom they identify and media such as the Internet, with which many young people feel very comfortable.

Most young people have very distinct opinions and ideas about their world and their futures by the time they reach their mid-teens, long before they are of legal voting age. Many of these ideas are, of course, shaped by hysterical or emotive media images. Not all parents have the experience or knowledge to

inform or counter those images, so schools may be the only places that can be expected to introduce issues in a calm, rational fashion which allows reasoned debate. However, they must be given the tools and support to do this, which requires an acceptance that it is an essential function which must be undertaken, despite the cost.

We have ignored the need to communicate with the majority of the population about our way of life and how it has shaped the landscape about which so many feel passionate. In consequence, we have failed to reach at least one generation completely. That generation is now making decisions about the future of rural Britain, frequently with no real understanding of the issues. They will not have to live with the consequences, be they financial, social or environmental. It is our responsibility to bridge that gap with the next generation.

Dawn Goodfellow has been Chief Executive of the Countryside Foundation for the last four years. Although her initial qualification was in Farm Business Management, she has spent the last ten years developing and managing projects linking education with business and the wider community. Dawn lives in the South Pennines, with her husband and three children.

It should be understood that the Countryside Foundation, of which Dawn Goodfellow is Chief Executive, supports education (especially of the urban population) about countryside matters, including aspects of country sports. However, as an independent charity, it does not associate itself with any particular 'cause'.

Access

Jonathan Young

'The Right to Roam' is a snappy phrase – far neater than 'The Right To Remove Other People's Right To Decide Who Walks All Over Their Land'. The difference in the phraseology is little more than sophistry and defines the access debate.

Ms Street-Porter, president of the Ramblers' Association, declares that "a freedom to roam over moors, mountains, heaths and downs should be treated as a fundamental human right and enshrined in law" and "not dependent on the whim of landowners who are lucky enough to hold property rights over our wild country". It is perhaps best to resist asking how Ms Street-Porter would feel about public access to her property, ie her house, and instead concede that her views do represent a body of opinion, albeit stridently expressed.

Faced with a vista of mile upon mile of open moorland it does seem absurd to keep it all for the sport of a chosen few. Why should the people be deprived of enjoying their nation's most scenic countryside just so an elite can enjoy ten weeks' shooting? The Ramblers apparently have a point. But they miss the main one, because it is not political but environmental.

Wildlife thrives where the public is not allowed. This is recognised by the new conservation landowners such as English Nature and the Royal Society for the Protection of Birds, both of which restrict public access to their reserves. Another prime example is the Ministry of Defence's land.

"Faced with a vista of mile upon mile of open moorland it does seem absurd to keep it all for the sport of a chosen few"

However, these institutional landowners' holdings are minuscule compared to those in private hands; it is the ordinary estate owner and farmer on which the future of Britain's wildlife depends.

The members of the Moorland Association manage over 600 000 of the estimated 700 000 acres of heather moorland remaining in England and Wales. It is denial to these acres that the Ramblers find particularly vexing and which Labour has in mind when it promises more national parks "under the control of independent boards... drawn from elected local politicians".

Moorland Association members have seen the chronic erosion caused by walkers to the Pennine Way and are anxious to preserve their moors from similar damage. They point out that those areas over which the Ramblers wish to roam are not usually arable and so have been spared the cocktail of herbicide, insecticide and nitrates that have destroyed much of the floral and animal diversity elsewhere. They are, then, of extreme national importance, with much of the heather moorland being designated a Special Protection Area; specifically, the Berwyn Mountains in north Wales comprise the largest Site of Special Scientific Interest in Britain.

Birds, especially ground-nesting species, are particularly reliant on these heather uplands. In one Pennine dale, Baldersdale, a RSPB survey found 318 pairs of curlew, 1165 pairs of lapwings, 187 pairs of redshanks, 97 pairs of oystercatchers, 24 pairs of golden plover and 12 pairs of black grouse. The rich array of smaller birds and mammals also supports the raptors; 20% of Europe's merlin population inhabits the north Pennines Area of Outstanding Natural Beauty.

This data comes from the RSPB but is widely promulgated by the Moorland Association, which presents a vigorous case for restricted public access. Organisations like the RSPB, with a membership of 890 000, have to be more circumspect, though broadly they encourage greater public access while duty-bound to put wildlife first.

In March 1995, the RSPB produced a report for a House of Commons Select Committee entitled *The Environmental Impact of*

Leisure Activities. This clearly refuted some of the walkers' more extravagant demands: "We do not believe access should be enhanced through introduction of a general 'right to roam' as this would establish an inflexible public right that would be difficult to alter in light of adverse impacts on biodiversity." It continues: "In cases where it is unclear as to whether enhanced access would have an unacceptable impact on biodiversity, then the precautionary principle should apply, and the benefit of the doubt be given to nature conservation. Where there is conflict between management for wildlife and management for visitors, management for wildlife takes precedence."

Visitors affect ground-nesting birds by causing them to leave the eggs or chicks to chill, or to desert them altogether. Dogs off leads are an especial menace. As Hugh Oliver-Bellasis, a conservation-minded landowner, says: "You do not get a second chance when the lapwing is put off her nest by a spaniel running wild." In addition, when birds are

flushed, their position is revealed to sharp-eyed avian predators, especially gulls and corvids. The report notes that "most of the remaining breeding populations of ringed plovers in southern and eastern England are now restricted to areas such as nature reserves that are protected from human disturbance".

To balance the demands for greater public access with the overriding need to protect wildlife, the RSPB, the Moorland Owners and the Country Landowners' Association have been striving to find the middle path, with voluntary access agreed at a local level. Landowners argue that·in many instances the footpaths are no longer relevant, since the destination to which these paths often lead is no longer important; for example, a church which has been sold. And frequently, these footpaths cross farmyards filled with heavy farm machinery, leaving the farmers facing legal liability should a walker be injured. They would prefer to establish new paths that allow recreational walking without undue disturbance but have found that such applications all too often bring the existence of the established footpaths to a bloody-minded element, which block any dissolution of the existing right of way and increase its usage to establish the point.

Nonetheless there have been successes. Paul van Vlissingen is owner of the Letterewe estate, a Highland deer forest of extraordinary beauty in Western Ross. Together with the Ramblers' Association of Scotland and other recreational groups, van Vlissingen drew up the Letterewe Accord in 1993 which many saw as the model for managing access. Visitors are welcomed, though they are encouraged to stay on the footpaths and come in small groups. Mountain bikes are discouraged.

As with most deer forests the majority of the stalking is done between September 15 and November 15 and visitors are asked to contact the estate office during this period for advice. It is explained to them that a single figure on a skyline or upwind of a parcel of beasts can ruin the stalking and seriously hamper the efforts to establish the target cull figure.

The estate also does its best to educate the public on wider concerns of deer welfare. And here, to quote The Red Deer Commission, there is a general 'communication problem': "most hillwalkers do not realise that by continually disturbing deer they are causing deer welfare problems. Deer have a well-ordered daily feeding, resting and ruminating cycle. If this cycle is being continually broken, the performance of deer stocks is affected. This is particularly serious in winter time when there are low or even negative feeding thresholds and winter death rates can rise steeply as the winter and spring progresses".

So far, the Accord has worked well, though van Vlissingen stresses that "certain places at certain times cannot tolerate visitors, in the same way that people sometimes do not want to be disturbed at home. In the case of the wild, it is the bird which is breeding on the loch shore, it is the eagle, it is the deer when they are managed through stalking".

Also, Letterewe is wonderfully isolated, with access mainly by foot or boat. The Accord makes a virtue of this and encourages visitors to "take the long walk in", stressing the need for "adequate experience, training and equipment to meet the rigours of travel in this remote area". No sign of an ice-cream van here.

On the moorlands it would be a very different story. Easy vehicle access there would open up the area to thousands of people, and the landowners would have to pay the cost of maintaining paths. This is a problem that has faced the RSPB at reserves such as South Stack, Holyhead, where some 100 000-plus visitors a year have eroded paths which have had to be repaired using local materials. In sensitive wetland areas, such as Fowlmere in Cambridgeshire, boardwalks have had to be constructed. The RSPB can afford this; many landowners cannot — and the maintenance of public footpaths fall on them, with extreme reluctance from the Ramblers to accept that there may be a case for their members paying for their pastime.

Even so, many moor owners would be prepared to meet the demand for access by providing "a variety of walks to meet established popular demand". What they will not do is allow unrestricted freedom to the moors at certain periods and close them during the nesting and grouse-shooting seasons. The reason is straightforward.

Grouse presently fetch £70 per brace on the sporting market and generate all the revenue needed for a moor's upkeep, which includes regular burning and predator control. Without this income, the moor would be put to other financial usage, such as sheep farming or forestry,

neither of which is environmentally beneficial – unlike shooting, an apparent paradox which is understood and supported by the RSPB but which defeats the League Against Cruel Sports and many urban-dwellers.

Were moor owners to notify publicly when they were shooting, the consequences would be inevitable – they would be targeted by hunt saboteurs. This has been a worsening problem in the past five years and would become acute if hunting were banned and the hunt saboteurs stuck to their pronounced intention to stop shooting next. To ask moor owners to provide saboteurs with venues and shoot dates is clearly absurd. For the Labour Party to promise the dilution of the legislation stopping aggravating trespass indicates dangerous naivety on this issue – but then they are still promising to "institute a right to roam".

This is no longer the demand of the Ramblers – despite the clarion calls of Ms Street-Porter, their president. A general right to roam is dismissed by George Hill, their press officer, as "an impractical thing". Instead, their chairman, Kate Ashbrook, now talks of her "vision of a countryside where people have the freedom to walk peacefully on open country – ie unenclosed, uncultivated land – provided they do no harm. Such access would be subject to commonsense restrictions to protect flora and fauna, archaeology, etc, and the interests of farmers and landowners". There is little here that would disturb most landowners, so long as the all-important qualifying conditions were kept.

"vision of a countryside where people have the freedom to walk peacefully on open country"

More worrying perhaps is Ms Ashbrook's second aim, that "where public subsidies are paid to landowners and land managers to take land out of production or to plant woodlands, there should automatically be public access, subject to the commonsense restrictions mentioned above". Here Miss Ashbrook correctly identifies a fissure running through the defence of those that would make no further concessions to walkers. The European Common Agricultural Policy – which created set-aside – has been of enormous benefit to many farmers, but how many of them, in accepting the payments, have pondered on that old adage, 'He who pays the piper calls the tune'?

"Get off my land" hardly has the same ring when the taxpayer is subsidising it especially when the land is covered in little but weeds.

Certain places at certain times cannot tolerate visitors – the same way that people sometimes do not want to be disturbed at home

The time for a very British compromise has come, with commonsense replacing the shouting for 'rights'. Otherwise the future for the countryside looks rather unhappy. As the owner of the Balavil Estate put it: "What's the point of owning a private piece of land when there are 45 walkers passing it every five minutes?"

Jonathan Young is editor of The Field

This Land is Your Land
Frederick Forsyth

L ike most of the contributors to this book, I too have travelled widely. From the snows of the Arctic to New Zealand's Bay of Islands; from Southend to Bantry Bay... via Yokohama.

I say this not to boast but to indicate that I have seen many countrysides and many landscapes, so that when I speak of this land of ours and its myriad beauties I can do so from a point of objectivity.

There is something about this landscape of rural Britain that is quite incomparable, unique to the planet. It is not its antiquity, although it has seen many centuries, for there are older landscapes; nor is it the variety of vistas available to greet the eye.

The uniqueness lies, I believe, in the sheer care that has been lavished upon it and still is. And yet, as Sir David Steel pointed out earlier, it is a landscape under threat. Why should this be?

Sir David hit upon the quintessence of the threat without delay; there exists an appalling and frightening ignorance of this great British treasure, an ignorance entertained principally by those who live in the towns and cities of our country.

Let me therefore continue by addressing the townspeople and city dwellers, and the media who represent yet largely misinform them.

A hundred years ago, 50% of the people of Britain lived in, and were a part of, the rural countryside – meaning that they dwelt in small market towns, villages, hamlets, manors and farms. The other half

"The uniqueness lies... in the sheer care that has been lavished upon it"

occupied the larger towns, suburbs and cities. Today the figures are radically different: over 80% live in towns and cities and less than 20% upon the land.

With the change in demography, political power has passed massively to the cities. Very few parliamentarians today represent an exclusively or mainly rural constituency. The old shire knights have gone the way of the scythe and the wheatsheaf. Even apparently rustic constituencies now contain sprawling overspill housing estates whose denizens must be appeased and placated. Politicians are about power; if power lies in the city vote then that is the vote that will triumph.

Yet in the same period, and certainly over the last fifty years, there has also been a revolution in communication. Instant reports, instant pictures, instant moving images in glorious colour in the corner of all our sitting rooms should surely have given even the most sequestered city dweller an understanding of the landscape beyond the suburbs that his grandfather could never have.

Ironically, the reverse has happened. A hundred, and even fifty, years ago the townsmen had a far greater understanding of, and empathy with, the countryside of his own land than today. How can this be? The answer is simple: it lies in that same technology that brings the images without the explanation.

A hundred years ago townspeople were much 'closer' to the countryside in many ways. There were working horses and donkeys in the streets, stables behind every shop, chickens kept in backyards, and thriving livestock and produce markets in every town.

Fifty years ago the milk and the coal were delivered, the rubbish collected, by horse and cart. Cockneys emigrated to Kent and Essex to harvest the hops, strawberries, apples and pears.

A hundred years ago townsfolk felt the passing seasons, just like the farmers. In summer you sweated in wool vests, buttoned shirts, waistcoats and suits. No electric fans, no ice-makers, no air conditioning. In winter you huddled and shivered, piling on the woollens to keep warm, with roaring fires only for the rich. No back-boilers and certainly no central heating.

Fifty years ago we all ate the foods of the season. Winter was for swedes, parsnips, turnip and cabbage, summer for salads, raspberries and plums, autumn for apples. You knew then that eggs came from chickens and milk from cows – a recent school survey showed 10% of inner-city children had no idea where they came from, but thought monkeys, lions and wolves remained wild in England.

Today there are no seasons for you. A visit to Sainsbury's or Tesco will provide every fruit and

vegetable from any country in any season. Your ham is vacuum-packed, not cut from the bone, your eggs come in styrofoam not straw, and mangoes are yours in December.

Technology has immunised the city dweller from all the basic facts of life by which the countryside still has to live: from sowing and harvesting, tupping and lambing, flowering and fruiting, but most of all from that endless cycle of the giving and taking of life without which farm and forest cannot continue to exist.

So, Townsman, do you want them to continue to exist? If you rise from your non-feather duvet to a timer/rheostat-heated house, breakfast off packaged eggs, packaged bacon, packaged bread and packaged butter; if you climb into a packaged car with heater at full blast, to drive between concrete walls to a central-heated office block, do you really want us to have a countryside at all?

Now, here is the rub. For opinion polls show quite clearly that over 80% of the British people, which must include 60% of townsfolk, claim they love and appreciate the British countryside. As well you may.

For it is remarkable. What we have here is far and away the most wildlife-rich rural environment in Europe. You speed through the countryside in your sealed car or speeding train, cosseted by warmth and muzak, look out at the landscape flashing by and, according to the polls, you like what you see. Here is another idea.

Take a light aircraft or look down from the window of your descending airliner. What lies beneath you is a patchwork quilt of every shade of green and brown, of fields and paddocks, leas and meadows, dotted with sheep and cows, pushing up their crops of wheat and barley, maize and rye, pea and bean. You are looking down at the five types of our countryside – woodland, arable, grassland, wetland and moorland. And, yes, you are quite right, it is beautiful.

And it is yours. To visit, to roam, to ramble, to saunter, to picnic. Even better, it is free. For most things in life you will be charged a licence fee or admission charge, but this incredibly beautiful land is free for you to enjoy. All we who live and work in it ask is: please take care of it and try to understand it.

A simple question. Do you really think all this came about by accident? Of course not. It came about because for three hundred years the yeoman farmers and estate owners have been sowing and reaping, trimming and pruning, cutting and lopping, digging and building, repairing and painting. The fields and woods alive with birds and animals, such a contrast to Europe with its songless forests, came about because for centuries the gamekeepers and foresters tended and nurtured their charges, breeding and releasing to the wild, controlling the vermin, clearing the deadwood, digging out the ditches, opening the culvert, planting new trees.

…looking down at the five types of our countryside –

woodland

arable

grassland

wetland

moorland

More simple questions. Does it cost? Of course it costs. Your rural landscape is the biggest garden in Europe, providing beauty, recreation and food. It costs hundreds of millions a year to maintain. So who pays? Well, not you Townsman. If the landscape of Britain had to be maintained out of public funds, you would have to see twenty pence in the pound added to your tax bill.

So who does pay for it all? Well, actually we do, the people of the countryside. Yes there are modest (more modest than you think) subsidies to the farmers, but they come from Brussels and we pay far more to Brussels than we get back. And there are grants-in-aid from the Treasury for certain projects, but a tiny fraction of the grants accorded to the cities. For the most part the hundreds of millions of man-hours needed every year to keep our countryside beautiful are put in by the farmers and landowners. Not because there is any money in it for them. It is a matter of pride, as a gardener will tend his lawn and a housekeeper paint his door.

And still the countryside is under threat as never before. Grossly inappropriate legislation from a largely and increasingly ignorant Parliament is part of the problem. Transmigration of young people who need a career and affordable housing, replaced by wealthy commuters and retirees, is another. Savagely slanted representation by journalists and programme-makers is a third, and shrill attacks on rural ways by single-issue fanatics is a fourth.

But the big threat, for it underpins the others, is the ignorance that has been allowed to develop among the 80% city-dwelling majority towards this national treasure. The countryside is neither a honeysuckle-wreathed chocolate-box cover, nor a charnel house populated by sadists, nor a soft option existing on subsidy handouts, nor an ecological coincidence.

This countryside of yours is multi-functional as well as good to look at. It provides 50% of your fresh food. It plays host to a wildlife pool of awesome variety but also of hair-trigger delicacy where humans exist in a harmony profoundly envied by our European neighbours with animals, birds and fish.

Despite the gloomy tone of some of the above, there are actually grounds for optimism. For years the countryside has been content to abide by the adage 'Never excuse, never explain'. Those days are long gone. Headed by organs like the Countryside Movement, the rural vote has realised that in this day and age it must explain that in the landscape every cause has an effect and every effect a cause.

Slowly, I believe, the case for the countryside is being made, not by shrill assertion but by reasoned explanation. Townspeople are beginning to realise that there is no 'you' and 'us' in this matter, for the landscape of Britain is part of all our heritage.

It is too valuable to all of us to be turned into weed-patch, car-park, tip or desert by the too-shrill voices of trendy ignorance.

Frederick Forsyth was born in the (then) small market town of Ashford, Kent, between the Weald and Romney Marsh, in 1938. Much of his boyhood was spent in and around the farmland that then encircled Ashford.

He began to travel in his early teens, becoming fluent in French, German and Spanish. After service in the RAF, he resumed his lust for travel as a correspondent for Reuters and the BBC. In 1970 he tried his hand at a novel and produced The Day of the Jackal, *subsequently leaving journalism to write full-time. He continues to travel widely, having visited almost 50 countries, and eight years ago fulfilled his own dream of buying a working farm, on which he now lives, in Hertfordshire. Apart from travelling, reading and writing, he also enjoys farming, shooting and fishing.*

Countryside Organisations

Deirdre Shields

T**here** are any number of countryside charities, organisations and pressure groups lobbying for our support and money. While we may not have anything in the UK to compete with America's "World Women For Animal Rights/Empowerment Vegetarian Activist Collective", these cover all subjects and shades of opinion. Or they should. One of the saddest things country people face is the realisation that you have to be the right sort of country person these days, even when it comes to giving to charity. Practising field sports, for a start, puts you beyond the pale.

If this sounds extreme, it is because animal/countryside politics have become ever more polarised. You are on the side of the angels, or you are damned; it is as simple as that. Issues are dealt with in black and white, and this, ironically, has coloured everything. We all seem to have been sucked into this, and the charities are no exception. Why should enjoying country sports and caring about animals be deemed mutually exclusive?

There seem to be such a plethora of organisations who profess to be working for the countryside that you may have wondered whether we are really marshalling our forces effectively. We have needed for a long time to establish one body that can speak for all the different interest groups committed to serving our countryside. This was finally set up last year. The **Countryside Movement** now provides a united lobbying and campaigning organisation representing all legitimate countryside interests as an holistic broad church. By the middle of 1996, after only six months in existence, it had achieved a figure of over 100 000 supporters on its database, with a target of over 250 000 by the end of 1996 and hopefully 500 000 in the course of 1997. It is non-political and welcomes donations from all bodies or individuals who care for the preservation of the British countryside and the rural way of life. Its Executive Chairman is Sir David Steel, its General Secretary Alex Armstrong, and Head of Policy Melinda Appleby. It operates from 11 Tufton Street, London SW1P 3QB (Tel 0171 233 1570, Fax 0171 233 1571) where all donations should be sent. They will be gratefully received.

We have also suffered from not knowing which countryside bodies were genuine organisations committed to serious programmes of preserving the traditional face of the countryside and which were more political lobby groups.

Most of the big charities keep their heads below the parapet, on the subject of field sports. The Worldwide Fund for Nature (UK) says: "WWF does not condone or condemn bloodsports… Bloodsports is essentially an animal rights issue, and as such we take no position although we are, of course, averse to anything involving cruelty or unnecessary suffering to animals." Greenpeace says "It's not an environment issue, better speak to someone at the League Against Cruel Sports". Some are more open than others.

Care for the Wild, for instance, is very direct: "We have no problem with indigenous hunting for food or subsistence, but are entirely against any form of hunting, even trophy hunting, for sport."

Field sports are part of the countryside. How can any charity that involves the countryside, however broadly, yet denies this fact, be said to represent the countryside in its entirety? The countryside needs all the help we can give. The following, then, is a practical guide to some charities that seem to have the interest of the whole countryside at heart, and which are sensible – even charitable – enough to put their cause above all else.

Two bodies which must head this list if you are a participant in or a passive supporter of field sports are the British Field Sports Society and the British Association For Shooting and Conservation.

The **British Field Sports Society** (BFSS), 59 Kennington Road, London SE1 7PZ (Tel 0171 928 4742) aims to ensure the retention of field sports as an integral part of the activities of modern society and to show how field sports enrich and conserve the wildlife of our country. They have 70 000 individual members and 400 000 affiliated members. A range of subscriptions are offered. Tarred for some years with being too 'county' an organisation that failed to reach the mass of field sportsmen who fished or did a bit of rough shooting, the BFSS has recently modernised its image dramatically. A new director, the well-known conservationist Robin Hanbury-Tenison, has gripped the organisation and has recently very successfully defused the worst excesses of a Parliamentary Private Members' Bill.

The **British Association For Shooting and Conservation** (BASC), Marford Mill, Rossett, Nr Wrexham, Clywd LL12 0HL (Tel 01244

570881) was formed by an amalgamation of the Wildfowlers' Association of Great Britain and Ireland (WAGBI) with the Gamekeepers' Association. It has a membership of 112 000 and is the governing body for sports shooting in Britain. It seeks to further the interests of the sport, setting and maintaining standards of sportsmanship, and to foster a practical interest in the countryside, wildlife management and conservation. Very importantly they run The Gamekeepers' Welfare Trust, and a large number of training courses.

Other bodies that deserve support are as follows:

Action with Communities in Rural England (ACRE), Somerford Court, Somerford Road, Cirencester, Glos GL7 1TW (Tel 01285 653477). ACRE takes the view that "any sport in the countryside is a community event, and is concerned with the rural community." An affiliation of 38 different local charities, ACRE works to promote initiatives in the countryside, be they village shops, community transport schemes or childcare facilities, along with other practical schemes. As a national campaigning charity, ACRE speaks out on countryside matters, from affordable housing to rural crime. Currently involved in a two-year campaign on rural poverty.

Atlantic Salmon Trust (AST) Moulin, Pitlochry, Perthshire PH15 5JQ (Tel 01796 473439). The AST is "neutral on hunting, and does not want to get involved with the arguments, but supports field sports generally." Dedicated to 'the well-being' of the wild Atlantic salmon, the AST tries to increase public awareness of the problems facing salmon.

While avoiding getting entangled in the arguments between netsmen and anglers, the Trust nevertheless promotes the view that salmon should be cropped in their rivers of origin "– and not elsewhere". Subscribers are invited to give "as little or as much as they can afford".

The **Badminton Trust**, Stone Cottage, Stockerston, Nr Uppingham, Leics LE15 9JD (Tel 01572 823448). The Badminton "Conservation and Educational Trust for the Countryside", to give its full title, points out that much woodland was planted for field sports. Set up in 1986, "to protect woods and spinneys and to make sure that they remain part of our landscape heritage," the Trust buys woodland for future generations. Replanting and education are its other two aims. Unusual in that it actively encourages field sports, the Trust aims to show that woodlands "are not static, but living, changing places which need skilful management". The Friends Scheme costs £25.

The **Barn Owl Trust**, Waterleat, Ashburton, Devon TQ13 7HU (Tel 01364 653026). Dedicated to that lovely creature the barn owl, the Trust offers free advice on all aspects of barn owl conservation, including habitat, nest boxes and barn conversions. Leaflets cover everything from *Indoor Nestbox Design* to *Sexing Barn Owls*. The Trust operates a Friends Scheme costing £15.

British Hedgehog Preservation Society, Knowbury House, Knowbury, Ludlow, Shropshire SY8 3LQ (Tel 01584 890287). "The Society does not have an opinion on hunting, so long as it doesn't harm hedgehogs." There is little doubting where priorities lie with this

Society. Staunch champion of the hedgehog, the Society takes a dim view of hedgehog jokes and works both to make the public more aware of hedgehogs, and give advice on their care (there is a helpline), as well as funding research on hedgehog behaviour.

British Isles Bee Breeders' Association, 11 Thomson Drive, Codnor, Ripley, Derbyshire DE5 9RU (Tel 01773 745287). Aimed, as the name suggests, at breeders, this educational charity encourages people to use indigenous bees, and works for the British bee – still having a rough time in the wake of the varroa virus. Offers advice for beekeepers.

British Trust for Conservation Volunteers, 36 St Mary's Street, Wallingford, Oxon OX10 0EU (Tel 01491 839766). The Trust is the largest practical conservation charity, involved in projects from pond-clearing to creating city wildlife gardens, and looking after cemeteries: "If it isn't practical, we don't do it." There are 10 000 members and 84 000 volunteers.

Butterfly Conservation, PO Box 222, Dedham, Colchester, Essex CO7 6EY (Tel 01206 322342). Engagingly enthusiastic on their subject, Butterfly Conservation think "coverts managed for hunting or game are also good for butterflies". According to Butterfly Conservation, butterflies "are the fastest declining group in the UK". Membership has rocketed in the last six years from 3500 to almost 12 000. Dedicated to saving our wild butterflies, moths and their habitats, if you care about the High Brown Fritillary or Adonis Blue, this is the organisation to get in touch with. There is a big campaign running on woodland butterflies, and volunteers are invited to record and map butterfly distributions for their project 'Butterflies For The New Millenium'. Membership costs £20.

The Country Trust, Stratford Grange, Stratford St Andrew, Saxmundham, Suffolk IP17 1LF (Tel 01728 604818). The Trust organises and conducts day- and week-long educational expeditions for children from inner-city areas. Visits encompass farms, forests, moors, lakes, rivers, estates and all kinds of rural businesses not usually open to the public. "The children learn a tremendous amount about the basic structure on which our food, farming and environment depend."

Countryside Education Trust, John Montagu Building, Beaulieu, Brockenhurst, Hants SO42 7ZN (Tel 01590 612340). Works to provide education "through stimulation and participation" in conservation, ecological and architectural projects. The Trust has a base on the Beaulieu estate and an 'Out of Town Centre' on a farm, which provides opportunities for people to get their hands mucky down on the farm.

The **Countryside Foundation**, Dean Clough Industrial Park, Dean Clough, Halifax HX3 5AX (Tel 01422 344555). An educational charity, the Foundation aims, without being patronising, "to research and provide information, knowledge and insight for a largely urban-based population about the relationship with, and effect of, country pastimes, leisure activities and sports on agriculture, wildlife and the rural environment and economy". The Foundation's pack for school children, *The Lychford File*, impressed *Blue Peter* presenter Diane-Louise Jordan.

The **Countryside Restoration Trust**, Barton, Cambs CB3 7AG (Tel 01223 843322). Almost worth joining for chairman Robin (*One Man and His Dog*) Page's irreverent newsletter. Apologising for the Christmas Draw ("I do not like draws, it is simply that the finances of it make such good sense") he admitted he "liked the second prize better than the first". Page believes the deterioration of the general countryside must be halted and reserves are not the answer. Set up in 1993 to show farmers could "farm profitably and still have wildlife and attractive landscapes", the Trust bought and replanted 40 acres of monoculture, and is raising money to buy a complete farm. Membership costs £10.

Dry Stone Walling Association, YFC Centre, National Agricultural Centre, Stoneleigh Park, Kenilworth, Warwickshire CV8 2LG (Tel 0121 378 0493). Persevere in the face of their stonewalling on the telephone, and you will find this is the body to provide everything you ever wanted to know about walling. Aimed at the amateur and craftsman, the Association offers advice on all aspects of the craft, and everything from beginners' kits to technical leaflets on *Specifications for Welsh Clawdd Walls* (bilingual). Open membership costs £9.

Earthwatch Europe, Belsyre Court, 57 Woodstock Road, Oxford OX2 6HU (Tel 01865 311600). Earthwatch provides scientific research by giving members of the public the chance to work as research assistants. They pay, and the money funds the projects, which vary from archaeological digs and health care in Africa to studying wolves in the Polish forests. "We are not a confrontational, or campaigning, organisation."

Forestry Trust for Conservation and Education, The Old Estate Office, Englefield Road, Theale, Reading, Berkshire RG7 5DZ (Tel 01734 323523). This charity seeks to redress the "Baddies Buying Up Blocks of Dark Conifers" image which forestry still has with some people. The Trust aims to promote forestry's wide-ranging role, through practical demonstration of "enlightened forest management", and show productive forestry can enhance wildlife and landscape. Started an individual membership scheme last year.

The **Game Conservancy Trust**, Burgate Manor, Fordingbridge, Hants SP6 1EF (Tel 01425 652381). Particular projects include: developing practical techniques for ensuring reared pheasants act more like their wild counterparts; using set-aside positively for conservation of species (eg partridges); promoting a greater understanding on the impact predators have on red grouse; encouraging innovative conservation measures for elusive game species; and game management for wild brown trout.

The **Hawk and Owl Trust**, c/o Zoological Society of London, Regent's Park, London NW1 4RY. Founded in 1969 to help save the peregrine, the Trust is committed to all birds of prey. Particular projects include hen harriers and long-eared owls. "The Trust believes that the best way to secure the long-term survival of birds of prey and their habitats is to harness the enthusiasm and support of those who own, manage or work the land."

Marine Conservation Society, 9 Gloucester Road, Ross-on-Wye, Herefordshire HR9 5BU (Tel 01989 566017). The Society is concerned "not just with things in the water", but all aspects of marine and coastal conservation. "We are not a militant organisation, we prefer to persuade." Compiles *The Good Beach Guide* for Reader's Digest. Membership costs £15.

Rare Breeds Survival Trust, National Agricultural Centre, Avenue Q, Kenilworth, Warwickshire CV8 2LG (Tel 01203 696551). It all began with a working party set up in 1968 by the Zoological Society and the Royal Agricultural Society of England. The Trust was founded in 1973 to assist native breeds of livestock (poultry came in later), through "advice, finance or moral support. 26 large breeds had become extinct during the twentieth century", but the tide has turned and breeds are flourishing. So is membership, which has grown from 200 to 10 000. 54 breeds are represented and there are programmes in 25 countries. Membership costs £15.

Royal Society for the Protection of Birds (RSPB), The Lodge, Sandy, Beds SG19 2DL (Tel 01767 680551). "Neutral on legitimate field sports", the RSPB has a staggering 890 000 members. The RSPB is focusing particularly on "decline in countryside birds, and farmland birds from the skylark to the lapwing". Membership £22 single, £27 joint.

The **Soil Association**, 86 Colston Street, Bristol BS1 5BB (Tel 01179 290661). Familiar to organic aficionados, the Soil Association has 4500 members and offers advice "and encouragement" to farmers. It is also concerned with "responsible forestry projects". The Vegetable Box

Scheme for consumers (vegetables delivered to the door and box collected once a week) costs £3.

Wildlife Habitat Trust, Marford Mill, Rossett, Clwyd LL12 0HL (Tel 01244 579881). Charitable wing of the British Association for Shooting and Conservation, the Trust raises funds to create, buy and manage wetland habitats, through its UK 'Duck' Stamp programme. This is based on a US idea, where hunting permits are validated with an annual stamp (a picture from a wildlife artist), with proceeds going to waterfowl and wetland conservation. Funds also go to international projects in Turkey, Estonia and Latvia.

Deidre Shields is a freelance writer. She is a regular contributor to The Field *and has written for, among others,* Shooting Times, The Daily Telegraph, The Times, Traveller, London Portrait, *and – much to her husband's embarrassment –* Brides & Setting Up Home. *She enjoys hill walking, beagling and pretending to fish.*

Photographs

Acknowledgements

With the exception of those listed below, all the photographs in this book were supplied by Simon Everett.

We would like to thank the following individuals and organisations for supplying additional photographs:

Source	Page references
Chris Bonington Library	66, 67, 68, 69, 70, 71, 73, 74, 75
Dawn Goodfellow	144, 146, 151b
Sophie Hill	54, 55
Alan Hinkes, Chris Bonington Library	72
Michael Honey	78
© Horse & Hound	52a, 52b, 53a, 57, 58a, 58b, 60
Robin Lowes	79, 83, 87
Nigel Luckhurst	81, 162, 170
Lizzie Orcott	59
Stewart Ross	118, 172a, 173b
Matthew Smith	16, 192
John Wilson	32a, 34a, 34b, 35b, 36a, 36b, 37a, 37b, 76

Our thanks also go to the contributors who supplied photos of themselves and:

• The BFSS for the photo of Robin Hanbury-Tenison on page 19
• Jim Meads for the photo of Michael Clayton, crossing Leicestershire with the Quorn Hounds, on page 51
• Ireneusz J Matusiak for the photo of Frederick Forsyth on page 167.

The photo of Nick Way on page 133 is © Belgrave & Portman Press Bureau.

Index to photographs

Note that where there is more than one photograph to a page they have been referenced a, b, c, etc from top to bottom and/or left to right.